GW00374828

THE FUNNIEST MAN ON EARTH

BOOKS BY GYLES BRANDRETH

Created in Captivity · A Royal Scrapbook · Yarooh!
I Scream for Ice Cream · Discovering Pantomime
Aladdin · Cinderella · Mother Goose
Brandreth's Bedroom Book

FAMILY ENTERTAINMENT BOOKS BY GYLES BRANDRETH

Brandreth's Party Games · Brandreth's Book of Waiting Games
Brandreth's Christmas Book
Brandreth's Complete Book of Home Entertainment
Games for Trains, Planes and Wet Days
Knight Book of Scrabble · Domino Games and Puzzles
Scrambled Exits: The Greatest Maze Book Ever
Teach Yourself In-door Games · Pears Family Quiz Book
Pears All the Year Round Quiz Book
The Generation Quiz Book · The Royal Quiz Book

CHILDREN'S BOOKS BY GYLES BRANDRETH

Knight Book of Party Games for Young Children
Knight Book of Christmas Fun · Knight Book of Easter Fun
Knight Book of Holiday Fun and Games
Knight Book of Hospital Fun and Games
Knight Book of Fun and Games for Journeys
Knight Book of Fun and Games for a Rainy Day
Knight Book of Mazes · Edward Lear's Book of Mazes
Knight Book of Home Entertainment
Fun and Games for Every Day of the Year
Number Games and Puzzles
Pencil and Paper Games and Puzzles
Games and Puzzles with Coins and Matches
Brainteasers and Mindbenders
Project: Castles and Historic Houses · Hotchpotch
The Great Big Funny Book · The Big Book of Secrets
The How and Why Bumper Wonder Book
The Second How and Why Bumper Wonder Book
Be Kind to Mum and Dad

GYLES BRANDRETH

The Funniest Man on Earth

THE STORY OF DAN LENO

HAMISH HAMILTON
LONDON

First published in Great Britain 1977
by Hamish Hamilton Ltd.
90 Great Russell Street London WC1B 3PT

ISBN 0 241 89810 2

Printed in Great Britain by
Western Printing Services Ltd., Bristol

To Saethryd

CONTENTS

ILLUSTRATIONS

The following pictures have been reproduced by kind permission of the Raymond Mander and Joe Mitchenson Theatre Collection:
1, 5, 6(a), 6(b), 6(c), 6(d), 7(a), 7(b), 7(c), 8(b), 9, 10(b), 11(a), 11(b), 12, 13, 14(a).

The remaining pictures, including those used on the jacket, are from the Leno Family Collection.

CHAPTER ONE

The Infant Wonder

1860 was the year of Gladstone's Free Trade Budget, of Dickens's *Great Expectations*, of George Eliot's *Mill on the Floss*, of some of the most famous paintings of Corot, Delacroix, Daumier, Degas, Vallon, Courbet and Manet, of the first Welsh Eisteddfod, of the invention of the telephone and the typewriter, and of the birth, at 4 Eve Court, in the Parish of Saint Pancras, London, of George Galvin.

Later 4 Eve Court was to become part of Platform One at Saint Pancras Station and George Galvin was to become 'the one and only Dan Leno', 'the funniest man on earth', 'the highest-paid entertainer of his day', 'a great genius'. However, Eve Court on 20 December 1860 was a far cry from the bright lights of Shaftesbury Avenue and Broadway. It was a tiny slum dwelling that contained two cold, damp, dismal rooms, rented for next-to-nothing by people who had next-to-nothing. The Galvins were itinerant entertainers. They lived a hand-to-mouth existence, earning a few shillings a week, performing in back-street pubs, fourth-rate theatres and the very cheapest music halls. They were known as 'Mr. and Mrs. Johnny Wilde' and billed as 'singing and acting duettists'.

The Galvins already had one son, a toddler called Jack, so, apart from being an extra mouth to feed, the arrival of baby George did not greatly affect their way of life. They went on travelling throughout the country, dragging the children and their handful of possessions with them, looking for work and taking it wherever they found it. When they arrived in a town and found themselves work at a pub or a hall, they set about looking for the cheapest digs: a room and a bed and a chest of drawers were all they needed. The parents and Jack would sleep in the bed. George would sleep in one of the drawers.

It was a hard life by any standards and so not altogether surprising that Mr. Galvin sought to alleviate some of its miseries with alcohol. What little money was left after the rent had been paid—and all too often *before* the rent had been paid—was poured down Mr. Galvin's throat. It was drink that drove him to an early grave. He died when little George was only four, leaving Mrs. Galvin a penniless widow with two sons to support. She struggled on alone, but not for long. Within a few months of her first husband's death, she had married her second.

When William Grant became head of the Galvin household, he took on his share of the burden, but he did not improve the family's lot. He too was an itinerant performer with a fondness for the bottle. He was of Lancashire stock, with Irish blood in him, and his stage-name was Leno. The life of the Grants was no more prosperous or glamorous than the life of the Galvins had been: the Lenos and the Wildes got about as many bookings. The new family carried on the tradition of the old, trudging from town to town, 'touring the smalls', the only difference being that the children now joined the act.

Dan Leno made his first professional appearance at the Cosmothica Music Hall in Bell Street, Paddington (now the site of the Paddington Baths) at the age of four. Billed as 'Little George, the Infant Wonder, Contortionist and Posturer', and dressed from top to toe in an old pair of his mother's black stockings, he postured, contorted and did a little dance his elder brother had taught him. Mrs. Leno was, of necessity, an ingenious improviser of costumes for her boys—she made Dan a smart suit out of an umbrella's silk lining and a handsome tweed jacket and Scotch cap from her old serge petticoat—and Jack was an able dancing master. By 1867, when George was still only six, the brothers were appearing together as a dancing double act.

In good weeks 'The Great Little Lenos', as the boys were billed, would appear at proper music halls, like the giant Britannia in Hoxton, which could seat over 3,000 people. In bad weeks—and there were many more bad than good—they would earn what they could busking outside pubs. The life of the unsuccessful variety artiste held no magic for Jack, and as soon as he was old enough he left the Leno troupe and went off to learn a trade. His place in the company was taken by his and George's uncle, Johnny Danvers, who was only a month older than his youngest nephew.

Johnny and George became firm friends. They shared everything, most especially a sense of humour. When they were not actually appearing together in public, they were performing for themselves, and though the routines they built up were thoroughly juvenile—they were only children, after all—some of their material—at least, as recalled by Dan in later years—was really rather funny:

DAN: I once had an IOU.

JOHNNY: So had I; but now I've only got U left.

DAN: Yes! Poor IO died.

JOHNNY: What did IO die of?

DAN: Don't you know? Iodide of potassium.

JOHNNY [*looking for socks and finding a pair with holes in them*]: Don't talk to me! I'm collecting my rents.

DAN: Ah! That's the worst of taking socks on a long lease.

JOHNNY [*inspecting socks*]: These are three quarters overdue! I must speak to my valet.

DAN: Oh! By-the-by, have you heard what's happened to *my* valet, Simpson?

JOHNNY: No! You haven't parted with him, have you?

DAN: I *had* to. He died.

JOHNNY: Of potassium?

DAN: No! A rattlesnake bit him in the Strand.

JOHNNY: It's a mean thing to do when a man isn't looking.

DAN: Oh! But the snake was perfectly fair. It gave him every chance. It rattled three times before it bit him.

In 1869, when George was eight, he made his debut as a solo artiste. The Britannia at Hoxton proudly announced the 'First appearance of the Great Little Leno, the quintessence of Irish Comedians'. Quite why or how he came to be billed as an Irish Comedian remains a mystery. Assuredly, there was some Irish blood on his stepfather's side of the family and perhaps Mr. Leno Senior felt an Irish comic would prove more popular than an English one. At any event, the Irish connection was further cemented the following year when George was billed for the first time as:

Dan Patrick Leno
Descriptive and Irish Character Vocalist

Whatever his billing, his act could only be described as 'Irish' in the most colloquial sense, since in his best-remembered turn he appeared as an Italian hurdy-gurdy boy. In this guise he sang a number called 'Pity the poor Italian' and had real, white rats crawling all over him as he sang. Inexplicably, this number was particularly popular in colliery towns.

Because the Leno family was booked as a whole and paid one salary, Mr. Leno had the ingenious idea of changing his step-son's name to 'Dan Patrick' in order to get him employed as a separate act with a separate salary. Dan Patrick's first recorded separate salary was a good one: twenty-three shillings a week, plus board and lodgings. As he later recalled, 'I never saw any of the twenty-three shillings, but I was allowed to keep the board and lodgings for my very own.'

While appearing on one part of the bill as Dan Patrick, he also continued to be a part of the 'Leno Family', whose stock-in-trade were comedy sketches with the emphasis on simple slapstick. One was called 'Torpedo Bill' and in it Dan played the title part. The sketch began with a comic cobbler (played by Mr. Leno) and his washerwoman wife (Mrs. Leno) in earnest discussion as to their mischievous son Bill's true vocation in life. The father wanted the lad to stick to his last. The mother was anxious for her son to better himself and saw him as a great inventor. The boy did his best to live up to his mother's fond wishes and invented a whole series of unlikely mechanical devices, each of which proved more disastrous than the one before, and the last of which brought the piece to a riotous climax, by blowing up the entire family. Dan played the title role in another sketch called 'Pongo the Monkey'.

This was one he particularly enjoyed, for apart from the fun of the Simian disguise, the business involved his chasing his stepfather round the stage and beating him soundly with a roll of brown paper. Given that Mr. Leno was not slow to beat his stepson off-stage, we can assume there was certain satisfaction for Dan in being allowed to beat his stepfather on stage.

If the Leno act does not sound too good, that is probably because it was not very good. Certainly, the demand for it was limited. 'Those early days were pretty bad 'uns,' Dan said when he was older. 'Misfortune met us round corners and got in our way at every turn. We went about singing in all sorts of places raising a lot of wind and a little money—fifteen shillings in a whole week at one time, thirty-five in one night at another—in all manner of ways. We were prepared to play anything, anywhere, at a moment's notice. I remember how we tramped once to a fair in Sutton-in-Ashfield, but art was evidently not wanted for we did not fare well. I recollect a manager in Stockport asking my father's advice as to what he should produce. It was Easter time, but my father replied without the slightest hesitation, "Produce a pantomime". We got into Stockport on a Saturday night, worked all day Sunday on the piece and produced it on Monday.'

Evidently Mr. Leno was a man of enterprise and initiative. When the family were in Sheffield, with their fortunes at a very low ebb, he chanced to see an advertisement that he fondly hoped might present the Leno troupe with the opportunity they had so long waited for and which had so unjustly eluded them heretofore. The nub of the advertisement was that an entrepreneur was wanted who could supply a really good high-class entertainment on the occasion of the festivities to be held in honour of the coming of age of the eldest son of a certain noble lord whose family seat was conveniently situated not twenty miles from Sheffield.

Since the fee offered was an inclusive one of fifty pounds, Mr. Leno sat down and sent off his letter of application at once. In it he stated that he, the great Leno, was an entrepreneur of immense experience and world-wide fame, that he was willing for the sum mentioned to bring down a company of London artistes, all of unrivalled ability and marvellous versatility, adding that the happy accident of this brilliant troupe being as close at hand as Sheffield was the reason that enabled him to offer his lordship such a unique entertainment for a mere fifty pounds. His company, continued Mr. Leno, was high-class or it was nothing, adding, of course, that where high-class was required it was simply and absolutely everything! Furthermore, Mr. Leno fearlessly undertook to supply any kind of high-class entertainment that his lordship might fancy—be it Light Opera, Comic Opera, Grand Opera, Shakespearean Revival, Farce, Orchestral Concert or Tragedy—but shrewdly concluding, 'If you wish to see my company at its very best, I would recommend a variety show as being our very strongest point.'

The letter brought the looked-for reply and on the appointed day, Mr. Leno and his distinguished company travelled by train to a small station down the line, where they were met by a wagonette and driven to the scene of the festivities. In later years, Dan took great delight in describing the members of the talented troupe:

1. The old man (Mr. Leno) got up as the entrepreneur. Hair well oiled, to the great detriment of his coat collar; shocking bad top-hat; and the inevitable Family Ulster with bits of an old fur boa of mother's stitched on the collar and cuffs.
2. A harmonium player, with a groggy face, carrying his harmonium.
3. A violinist who squinted.
4. A cornet player with four teeth out—the worst cornet player in the provinces.
5. A Negro comedian in a velvet coat and corduroy trousers.
6. The human eel. A very fat man with a purple face through bending backwards.
7. A lady vocalist, dressed entirely in stage 'props', and wearing a hat a man had once worn when he played Romeo.
8. Johnny Danvers in patched boots.
9. Dan Leno in frayed trousers. And

10. The luggage. An old tin box with hollows all over it, and tied up with pieces of rope.

When they arrived at their destination, they found that the entertainment took the shape of a garden party. A platform had been erected at the end of a lawn for their performance, and behind it stood a large marquee. Strolling about the lawn were ladies and gentlemen, all beautifully attired, and in order to reach their dressing-room, the company had to cross it in full view of the assembled guests. They hesitated a moment. Then Mr. Leno boldly took the plunge, and led the way. They were met on the other side by two flunkeys in gorgeous livery, before whom Mr. Leno, temporarily overawed, took off his hat and bowed humbly. The flunkeys, eyeing the party disdainfully, merely pointed to the marquee, and retired.

The players entered the marquee and were delighted to see, spread before them, a large round of beef, pickles of many varieties, and jugs of beer to wash it all down. For a moment they gazed in silent admiration. The human eel was the first to speak. 'Oh dear! I wish my poor wife was here!' he said. But not being a man to waste time over foolish and unavailing regrets, he heaved one sigh, philosophically remarked, 'Well, if she's not here, I am,' and tucked in to the spread. He showed such strong tendencies towards rapid consumption that the rest of the company had, in self-defence, to sit down without loss of time and join in the fray.

A somewhat prolonged meal was the result. Indeed, it was not until after five or six messages, each one more urgent than the last, had been sent by the steward to know if the company was nearly ready to begin the performance, that Mr. Leno reluctantly gave the word to desist. The human eel, who had been particularly heavy on the beer and pickles, sat back in his chair with a satisfied grunt, wiped his mouth with the back of his hand, and remarked somewhat huskily, 'Guv'nor! put me on last!' It was a pity, as it afterwards turned out, that Mr. Leno did not take this sound advice.

The proceedings opened with a performance of the overture

to the opera *Zampa* by the full orchestra. This was so distressingly bad that the audience took it to be intentionally so, and laughed heartily at what they imagined to be a burlesque of the real thing. The insulted orchestra retired, in high dudgeon, to the marquee, there to console themselves with more beef and beer, and Mr. Leno, remarking that if they wanted to laugh he would give them something to laugh at, turned on the black comedian instead of the lady vocalist, whose next turn it should have been.

This gentleman had a large stock of jokes from which to draw —jokes that were for the most part more distinguished for breadth than length, and that certainly possessed the merit of being absolutely new to a fashionable audience. The effect of them was instantaneous. At the end of the first joke a distinct shiver ran through the audience; the second caused them to shuffle their feet restlessly; the third emptied half the seats; and the fourth was never finished, because Mr. Leno, who knew the punchline, audibly insisted on the performer leaving the platform before he got more than half-way through.

The entrepreneur now felt that something must be done quickly in order to obviate disaster, so he decided to play his trump card. Mounting the platform, he announced to those who had bravely remained in their seats that he had much pleasure in introducing to them a most sensational novelty, none other than 'The Human Eel'. Applause, a chord from the band, and the human eel stepped on to the platform in the bright sunlight, attired in green tights, mended, in various places, with blue worsted.

'My first feat', said he, 'will be to bend backwards, pick up a glass from the ground with my teeth, and consume the contents as I resume my original position.'

Placing the glass on the ground, and sighing deeply, he began to bend, anxiously watched by the rest of the company.

He struggled nobly, until—there was a sharp rip, the green tights yielded where the blue worsted most predominated, and the remainder of the audience retired.

In vain, Mr. Leno remounted the platform, and entreated them to remain and see 'the great and only Dan Leno, the greatest dancer and comedian on the stage'. They knew when they had had enough, and publicly intimated the same. A brief period of doubt among the company as to what it was advisable to do next was peremptorily settled by the steward, who informed Mr. Leno that the further services of himself and his distinguished company would be dispensed with; that the wagonette was now waiting to take them back to where it had, unfortunately, found them; and that the cheque for £50 would be sent in the course of a day or two.

That was it. The company had little alternative but to board the wagonette and head for home. Several days elapsed, but there was no sign of his lordship's cheque. Since the troupe had already spent much of the fifty pounds in anticipation of receiving it, Mr. Leno decided to set out and collect the sum in person. When he arrived at the noble gentleman's estate he was informed that his lordship was out shooting. Mr. Leno tramped through fields and woodlands for a further four hours and eventually came upon the shooting party. His lordship explained that he was not in the habit of carrying fifty pounds about him on his person, but managed to give him seven on account, with a promise of a cheque in the post that very night. Mr. Leno thanked his lordship and began the weary trudge home. When he left his lordship's estate he had seven pounds in his pocket. When he reached Sheffield and the arms of Mrs. Leno he had three. In between times, it would appear, the mighty Leno had entertained most of the village at the local alehouse while waiting for—and missing—four trains.

The next morning, the promised cheque arrived, but it did little to alter the family's fortunes, for after the rest of the company had received their share, and the expenses already incurred had been paid, there were only a few pounds left and these Mr. Leno was able to dispose of with remarkable ease.

At the best of times, Mr. Leno was a man of fierce temper with whom only the bold chose to argue. In consequence, the private and professional life of the Leno troupe was not without its stormy moments. Dan used to tell the story of the time when the company had been engaged to appear for one night only in some hall in a small market town where the proprietor of the hall, having agreed to fit up a suitable stage and to provide decent furniture and fittings at his own expense, basely endeavoured, at the last moment, to back out of his share of the undertaking. When the afternoon rehearsal began, with the proprietor as an interested spectator, Dan's stepfather opened the proceedings by calling out, 'Dan, come on the stage to me!'

'My boy,' said his stepfather, 'I'm going to tell you what to do in this scene,' and, speaking *to* Dan and *at* the proprietor, he continued—

'When you come on the stage you will find me sitting just here on a chair (although Heaven alone knows if there will be any chair here for me to sit on). I will be resting my elbow on a table (of course, that's always supposing the wretched proprietor of this hall is not too mean to provide a table). You put your arm on my shoulder (I can guarantee that effect all right, Dan, because this poverty-stricken company of ours provides the arms and shoulders that are necessary in this piece) and you hand me a letter. (By-the-by, Dan, just before I go on, let me know if the management of this place grudge you a bit of paper for that letter. If they do, go out in the market-place and beg a bit, and tell everybody why you are obliged to do it.)

'I will jump up and go to a desk that will stand in this corner (at least, it won't stand anywhere if the mean hound who runs this hall has anything to do with it); out of the desk I will take a photograph (which, by the way, means more expense for the grasping management), and I will say, "Curse him!" (And if all the furniture and "props" aren't there in their places tonight, you'll know very well who I mean when I say it.)

'When I do this, you will stand there in the moonlight (although the Lord knows if there'll be any moon; some people are capable of grudging you the light of heaven), you will turn your face to the audience (and I'll bet there's no audience if they know anything at all about the skunk that owns this barn), and, just as you say, "Stay! He is your son!" the curtain will fall (and, when I say that, I'd like to lay long odds there won't be anything so expensive as a curtain provided for us here tonight)—'

Here the proprietor broke in at last. 'Yes,' he said, 'and after that you'll come round to collect the receipts, and from what I've seen of your performance so far, I'm open to bet my boots that there won't be any.'

Alas, the proprietor's prophecy was almost, if not quite, fulfilled.

Alcohol was the solace Mr. Leno sought in times of disaster. Whether the disaster was of a personal nature—yet another week and no work—or more general—the eruption of Vesuvius or a colliery explosion in South Wales—it hardly mattered: Mr. Leno consoled himself in just the same way. Inevitably his drinking came to affect his performance: on one occasion, in an almost fatal manner. Dan, Johnny Danvers and Mr. Leno were working what used to be called a 'double-trap scene' at a hall in Manchester. Johnny and Mr. Leno, dressed as demons, popped in and out of a room, up star-traps, down grave-traps, leapt through windows, while Dan, in the character of an Irishman, chased them vigorously.

Unfortunately Mr. Leno, who had been assuaging his grief in the usual way, miscalculated his distance and, in going down a grave-trap, hit his head hard enough to cut it open. Dan saw the accident he was unable to prevent, and stood on the stage alone, wondering what was going to happen next. There was a brief pause, and then up sprang Johnny through the star-trap with tears streaming down his cheeks.

'How's the dad?' whispered Dan, as he went for him with his shillelagh.

'He's killed,' replied Johnny, and dived down the grave-trap.

Dan, quite overcome, and unable to remain on the stage another moment, dived after, and fell on top of him.

Below they found Mr. Leno in a bad way, with blood streaming from the wound in his head; so without waiting to remove their make-up, or change their stage clothes, they got him into a cab and drove post-haste to the nearest doctor.

When the maid who answered the bell saw standing before her an Irishman and a demon supporting another demon with blood running down his face, she naturally shut the door again and fled shrieking. Alarmed by her outcries, the doctor himself put his head out of an upper window and surveyed the group with astonishment.

Some little explanation was required before he could be convinced that his weird visitors were of this world; but, in the end, they were admitted, Mr. Leno's injuries (which turned out to be not so bad as they appeared) were attended to, and the young Irishman took his two demons back to the hall to work another 'turn'.

Eventually, this 'young Irishman', his uncle and parents set sail for Ireland in the hope that the fortune that had eluded them in Britain might be theirs in the Emerald Isle. It wasn't. There was about as much work for the Lenos in Dublin and Belfast as there had been in London and Sheffield. This is how Dan struck someone who saw him on this first trip to Ireland:

> A smallish man, or a biggish boy, with an expression of chastened sorrow on his features, somewhat tempered by a mischievous twinkle in his eye. On his head a white billycock hat of the usual basin shape he always affected in those days (there is strong reason to believe it was always the same hat), a short coat, a still shorter waistcoat, with a considerable piece of vacant land between its termination and the beginning of the trousers.
>
> Item, a pair of elastic-side boots that were worn indifferently by Dan and his mother, and which fully accounted for the fact that, unless Dan wore his clogs, they were never seen out in the street together.

But even his clogs had hardly any sole to them. 'Walking on his uppers' was something Dan grew quite used to.

In Ireland Dan picked up the Irish lilt to his accent which he never lost and a compliment from Charles Dickens, who was in Belfast on one of his lecture tours and having seen Dan dancing went backstage to say to him, 'Well done, little man. You'll make headway.' But a 'bouquet' from a distinguished author and fifteen shillings a week were not much to live on, so the Leno family, having failed to find their Hibernian crock of gold, made their way back to England.

The poverty was real enough, but once he had made the 'big time' Dan never dwelt on the past 'nightmare of struggles and deprivations'. He preferred to recall the more amusing moments of the lean years of his youth: 'On one occasion our small company were to play at the Adelphi Theatre, Liverpool, and when we arrived, I hired a man with a hand-cart to convey our shabby and curiously assorted baggage to the theatre. An old tin tray tied in with string formed the bottom of one of the baskets, and altogether the barrowload looked like a one-room eviction. I told the man to take these bits and pieces to the "Adelphi", and then I went and bought some cakes, one of which I gave to some little girls, who licked off the jam and played hopscotch with the rest. Then I found the theatre, but no baggage.

'I spread myself over the town, and finally discovered the man, with an old bedstead (part of our "props") on his back, struggling with two liveried servants on the steps of the Adelphi Hotel in Lime Street. He had been told to take the things to the "Adelphi", and he would have them in if it killed him. It was indeed a sublime and noble sight. The face of the muddy street was covered with our belongings, for the basket with the tin tray had already fallen to pieces after being pitched from the hotel.

'And that same baggage caused a bucketful of trouble at the Britannia Music Hall, Sheffield. On our arrival, Mother and Father went lodging-hunting whilst I conveyed our 'props' to the theatre. I had to bore a hole in the stage in which to fix an upright that we used in the sketch we were playing. It was nearly dark, so I struck matches every few hours to see how I was going on. The boring finished, I went away for a moment to fetch something. On returning I found, to my horror, a light shining through the hole I had bored. "Great Caesar!" I thought, "I have dropped a match through the hole and set the stage on fire."

'Like lightning I flew to the dressing-room, seized a bucket of water, and rushed back to the stage. The light was brighter, and pouring every drop of water through the hole I waited with beating heart to see the result. It astounded me more than if the whole theatre had burst into flames, for this is what happened: a gruff voice under the stage exclaimed, "What ta devil is ta doin' oop thear? Does ta want ter drownd me?" I never left a theatre quicker. With great caution I afterwards learned that the proprietor's pony was stabled underneath the stage, and the man who came to look after it had (unfortunately) placed his neck in the best possible position for receiving my bucketful.'

When Dan Leno first went to Dublin he was paid fifteen shillings a week 'and jolly glad I was to get it'. When he went back he was paid £100 a week. 'I've earned a good deal of butter to my bread in my time,' he reflected at the height of his career, 'but I should have enjoyed it more if it had been better spread. I don't want to eat dry bread on Monday and lumps of butter on Saturday.'

CHAPTER TWO

Champion Clog-Dancer of the World

By 1880, when Dan was in his twentieth year, he had already spent the best part of sixteen years in the 'business'. Each of those years had been much like the last: a booking at the bottom of the bill in the good weeks, nothing but hunger in the bad. He had travelled, always with the family, never alone, to most parts of the kingdom, though for several years they were based in the Midlands or the North, making occasional forays to Scotland or the Home Counties and the one expedition to Ireland. They moved from one set of theatrical digs to another (Mr. Leno would write asking for 'a room for myself and my wife and any odd corner you may have for the boys') and sometimes even settled for a couple of months in a small rented house or flat, but none of them offered much by way of home comforts. They were poor, as they had always been, but it was not the grinding poverty of the destitute: it was the everyday poverty of the Victorian working class, the sort of poverty that Mrs. Leno stoically accepted as her lot, that Dan and Johnny Danvers dreamt of escaping from without really ever expecting to, that Mr. Leno managed to obliterate as often as possible in the time-honoured way.

But in 1880, for the first time, the family's fortunes did begin to change, thanks entirely to Dan's feet. Dan's elder brother Jack, who had left the troupe to learn a trade and died soon after, had taught Dan some basic steps when he was only five. As soon as the family moved to Lancashire to look for work, Dan had capitalised on his own natural nimbleness by learning to clog-dance. He rapidly became an expert clog-walloper, completely at home in the arcanum of what a supercilious southerner once called 'Northern working-class tap-dancing', executing the most complex steps—the rolls, kicks, taps, twizzles and shuffles—with ease and skill. He would boast, 'I can put more beats into sixteen bars of music than a drummer can with his drumsticks', and he was probably telling the truth.

When Dan Leno clog-danced he did not have a set routine: he was a firm believer in 'extempore dancing' and so every time you saw him in action you saw something slightly different. He could dance to almost any piece of music, though given the limited musical abilities of the bands at the halls and theatres at which he played in his youth, he was normally obliged to dance to the same piece of music. On one occasion he turned up for rehearsal at a small music hall in a manufacturing town in Lancashire armed with a medley of operatic airs, specially compiled and arranged by his stepfather, who considered himself something of an opera buff, and handed the band parts to the conductor proudly: 'This isn't the old stuff, this is something new.'

The conductor inspected the medley. 'By gum, this is something extra.'

'Rather,' agreed Dan proudly. 'There's some high-toned music among that.'

'There's lumps of it,' retorted the conductor, 'and, if I'm not mistaken there's going to be a bit of trouble over this job.'

He was not mistaken. The band made several bold attempts to play the new music and the new music most definitely lost.

'If you'll take a fool's advice,' said the despairing maestro, 'you'll leave this stuff alone and go back to th' good old la-tum-tiddle.'

But Dan was determined. His stepfather had produced some high-class clog-dancing music for him and he wanted to have it played.

'Look here, Mr. Leno,' the conductor concluded, 'we can't keep th' rehearsal waiting all day while me and my chaps is trying to find out what your new music is about. Let's pass on. I'll keep th' lads for a couple of hours after you've all gone, and you can tak' my word for 't as we shall get through it same as a band o' two-year-olds tonight.'

And sure enough, when Dan stepped onto the stage that night, the band played a rousing opening chord with *brio* and confidence—but it was not a chord that had anything to do with Mr. Leno Senior's fine operatic airs. After the chord came silence. And through the silence came the conductor's loud tones: 'It's no use, Mr. Leno, the lads couldn't tackle your job under a matter of three weeks, so that unless tha can be content with th' old la-tum-tiddle tha must dance wi'out ony music.'

So Dan danced that night to 'th' old la-tum-tiddle' and put away his stepfather's medley for good.

It was in Wakefield in 1880 that Dan first entered a proper clog-dancing contest. The prize was a purse of silver and a leg of mutton, and he won both the money and the meat with ease. Inspired by this success, and urged on by a friend of Mr. Leno's, a comic singer called Frank Belton, who fancied himself as something of a tipster in the world of competitive clog-walloping, Dan entered a competition at the Princess's Music Hall in Leeds, in which the first prize was a gold and silver belt, weighing 44½ ounces and valued at £50, *and* the right to the title of 'Champion Clog Dancer of the World'.

Although the competition was open to all-comers, the intention behind it was to bring together two long-standing rivals, Tom Robson and Tom Ward, both local favourites with enthusiastic and vociferous supporters very ready to put their money where their mouths were and back their man to the hilt. To nobody's surprise, the two Toms survived the preliminary heats, but so did young Leno. Indeed, to the amazement of all and disgust of many, the outsider not only survived the heats, but won every round, trouncing the two favourites, and carrying off the belt and the title in triumph.

Having become Champion Clog Dancer of the World, over the next couple of years he was regularly called on to defend his title. The first three of these title fights he won, but at the fourth, the judges found in favour of a rival dancer. 'I disputed the judges' verdict at the time,' said Dan later, 'but did not argue about it.' Others, however, did, no doubt encouraged by the irate Mr. Leno Senior. And judging from the tone of the bill produced at

Ohmy's Circus of Varieties in Accrington when Dan appeared there, he himself was not accepting his defeat altogether submissively:

> Little Dan's challenge for £400 a side remains unaccepted. This is open to the World. He will nightly expose the contest in which he was not allowed to win, after beating fifteen of the best dancers in the Kingdom. The present holder of the Belt would not stand his chance and dance a second time, according to the conditions of the champion contest, but preferred to buy the Belt of Mr. Mellon for the sum of £10. This fact will prove to the public who remains champion still!

The new champion, having preferred to buy the belt than defend his right to keep it, actually managed to lose it altogether! And it was not until May 1883 that another belt was fashioned and a fresh competition staged at the People's Music Hall, Oldham. This time, there were no disputes. Dan Leno took on all-comers and triumphed. The inscription on the belt was unambiguous—

CHAMPION BELT
WON BY
DAN LENO
CHAMPION CLOG DANCER OF THE WORLD
AT THE
PEOPLE'S MUSIC HALL, OLDHAM
AFTER SIX NIGHTS' CONTEST
MAY 14TH TO 19TH, 1883

—and he kept it until the end of his life.

His growing fame as a dazzling dancer and his undisputed ownership of the champion's belt were good for business. Not only did the number of bookings increase, but his billing improved as well. For example, when he appeared (not, in fact, for the first time) at the Britannia Music Hall in Glasgow, the bills proclaimed:

First appearance in Scotland of the Conquering Hero,
Mr. Dan Leno!
Champion Clog Dancer of the World.
He will appear nightly in his Champion Clog Dance.

1 Dan Leno in November 1902

2a Lydia Reynolds, 'comedy vocalist'

2b Dan Leno in 1883 with the belt of the Champion Clog Dancer of the World

3a Dan and Lydia in 1884 with baby Georgina and Lydia's parents, Mr. and Mrs. Reynolds of Rochdale

3b Dan and Lydia and their children in 1896
Top row: John William, Georgina Louisa, Sidney Paul;
second row: Ernest George, May Lillian, Herbert Dan

4a The Old Mo playbill
for 5 October 1885

MIDDLESEX
MUSIC HALL,
"MOGUL TAVERN," 167, DRURY LANE.
PROPRIETOR · · MR. J. L. GRAYDON.
MONDAY, OCTOBER 12, 1885,
AND EVERY EVENING.
FIRST APPEARANCE AT THIS HALL.
CHEEVERS
AND
KENNEDY,
THE FAMOUS BUFFALO BOYS.
Another Middlesex Favourite.
DAN LENO,
The Great Comic Vocalist and Champion Dancer of the World.
DON'T FAIL TO SEE HIM.
THE GREAT
ROMAH TRIO,
The most Sensational Horizontal Triple Bar Act before the Public.
NORA DARRELL
The New Irish Gem.
FRED COYNE,
IN ALL NEW SONGS.
EVA BELL,
The New and Pleasing Serio.
SAM REDFERN,
AS DROLL AS EVER.
PANDORA,
A PUZZLE FOR ALL.
O'CONNOR AND BRADY.
BOB & JENNY LEONARD.
SISTERS COLLINS.
ALICE WESTFIELD.
BROS. HARRISON,
The Clever Little Variety Artistes and Dancers.
MONDAY NEXT, OCTOBER 19th,
First Time at this Hall. A Sensational Entertainment, entitled THE
BRIDGE!
By POLLY RANDALL, CHARLES WILFORD, and EDIE FRENCH.
ENTIRE NEW SCENERY.
CHAIRMAN · MR. GUS. LEACH.

4b The Old Mo playbill
for 12 October 1885

5 The Baroness in *Cinderella* in 1895

6a A humble Mother Goose in 1902

6b A ravishing Mother Goose in the same production

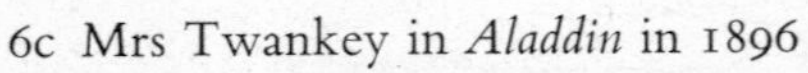

6c Mrs Twankey in *Aladdin* in 1896

6d Queen Spritely in *Humpty Dumpty* in 1903

7a Idle Jack in *Dick Whittington* in 1894

7c Dan and Herbert Campbell as Abdullah and the Fair Zuleika in *The Forty Thieves* in 1898

7b Dan and Herbert Campbell as Reggie and Chrissie in *Babes in the Wood* in 1897

8a Dan Leno, Johnny Danvers and Herbert Campbell

8b Dan and his harp in his dressing room at Drury Lane during the run of *Bluebeard* when he played Sister Anne

A week later he is still in Glasgow:

The audience nightly in rapture at the inimitable
dancing of Dan Leno,
Champion Dancer of the World,
In his Matchless Prize Hornpipe. Every Evening.

And the following week, he is still there:

Re-engagement for one week longer, by universal
request, of Dan Leno,
Champion Dancer of the World.

And, of course, further down on the same bill he reappears as part of the family troupe:

The Comic Trio (Mr. and Mrs. Leno and Dan Patrick)
In their really Funny Entertainments, Songs,
Dances.

The champion's belt was almost as prized by his employers as was the champion himself and whenever possible they mentioned it in the billing:

Still Champion of all the Champions,
Dan Leno,
Vocal Comedian and the World's Champion Dancer.
Holder of the only Legitimate Champion
Gold and Silver Belt,
The Grandest Piece of Workmanship
Ever produced in this Country
Cost £50.
One Week only.

When he went on stage as Champion Dancer of the World he always wore the belt and he was invariably accompanied by his 'Trainer' (a part usually taken by Mr. Leno Senior) who warmed up the audience by extolling the virtues and recalling the triumphs of young Dan. When the Trainer had concluded his fairly lengthy oration, Dan's belt would be removed, the Trainer would retire and the Champion would dance. He danced all over the stage, he danced on a pedestal, he danced on a slate, and he did it all without uttering a word. A dancer was expected to dance: in the North of England in the 1880s, no one wanted him to be funny as well.

Naturally, Dan's comic talents were still used to good effect when he appeared with the rest of the family, especially, apparently, in a 'most gorgeous spectacular entertainment' created by Mr. Leno Senior at about this time. The piece was called *The Wicklow Wedding, or The Leprechaun's Revels.* It was written by Mr. Leno, who also contributed an original song, with splendid scenery painted by Dan and lavish costumes made by Mrs. Leno.

When you consider what the little company had to provide at the Star Music Hall, Ancoats, Manchester on the occasion of 'The Benefit of the Leno Comic Quartette' (the foursome consisting of Mr. and Mrs. Leno and Dan, plus Johnny Danvers posing as Mr. H. Leno), you realise how hard they had to work for their modest living. In addition to a full performance of *The Wicklow Wedding* and some championship dancing from Dan, the Star's patrons were offered:

Five Grand Prizes given as follows:—
Purse of Silver for the finest Baby under twelve
months old.
Each child to be weighed on the stage, and the Mother
to appear with the child on the stage at
The Baby Show.
A Purse of Silver
For the best Amateur American
Song and Dance.
Purse of Silver
To the best Amateur Comic Singer.
A Purse of Silver
For the best Amateur Clog Dancer.
A Handsome Counted Collar
Will be given as a prize for the largest and most
handsome cat.
And to add to the gaiety of the night,

A Purse of Silver
To the exhibitor of
The Best Performing Elephant!

At another Benefit performance, this time at the Grand Varieties Theatre in Sheffield, Dan alone is billed as the beneficiary, but the 'extras' offered to the public were quite as spectacular:

> Mr. D. Leno intends to spare no expense to make this the most pleasant and enjoyable entertainment ever witnessed in Sheffield.
>
> Look at the following Eight Grand Contests and Double Company!
>
> Now come Leno's seasonable gifts:
> 200 Half-ounces of Tobacco
> To the first 200 entering the Pit and Side-seats.
> Every half-ounce genuine.
> Now come the contests:
> Ten shillings for the best Clog Dancer.
> Dan Leno, judge.
> Each dancer to dance six steps,
> And shuffle in good clogs.
> No person that has gained his living by dancing
> will be allowed to enter.
> Ten Shillings to the Lady and Gentleman that can
> waltz six times round the stage the neatest.
> Half a crown each
> Will be given for the longest standing jump,
> For the best singer of two verses of a
> Comic Song,
> For the best High-Kicker,
> For a Sack Race,
> For a Boot-Finding Contest,
> For the person that can stand on the side of a barrel
> and sing a verse of a song.

In 1880, the year in which he first won the right to the title of Clog-Dancing Champion of the World, Dan met Lydia Reynolds in Rochdale. In 1883, the year in which he secured the world title, he married her. She came from Sunderland and although only seventeen, she was already a seasoned performer and joined the Leno troupe as a 'comedy vocalist'. Their wedding, at Saint George's Church, Hulme, Manchester, was a modest affair. They had to walk two miles to get to the church and even the solitary bouquet of flowers was stolen. Just two friends came along with them and, according to Dan, the quartet felt like 'four little people sneaking into a big church through a back door'. Mr. Leno was too busy celebrating to actually witness the union and Mrs. Leno stayed at home to prepare the wedding breakfast: 'cold meat and potatoes, topped off with wedding cake made of bread puddings.'

Dan and Lydia, Johnny Danvers and Mr. and Mrs. Leno carried on much as before, with the Leno troupe and Lydia Reynolds remaining towards the bottom of the bill at the halls and theatres they visited and Dan on his own moving gradually towards the top. Eventually, the day came in 1885 when Dan was offered his first London engagement and decided that the moment had come to leave the troupe and make his way alone in the world. He was twenty-four and Lydia was nineteen.

When the young couple set off for London, the old couple as good as retired from the stage. Mrs. Leno used to boast that she completed fifty years as an active performer, but in truth her appearances after 1885 were rare. Dan was sorry to leave her behind, for he loved and admired her greatly. Hers had not been an easy lot and her fortitude in the face of life's ravages (and Mr. Leno's rages) was never forgotten by her grateful son. As soon as Dan was earning enough money to be able to spare anything, he sent it off to her, and once he began to prosper he took a house for both his mother and stepfather in the suburbs of Manchester and provided them with a pension that kept them in comfort until the end of their days.

Mr. Leno enjoyed his retirement hugely, spending most of it in lowly alehouses and hostelries. When Dan made one of his periodic visits to his parents following his success—they did not come to town to see him and he did not encourage them to do so —Mr. Leno would insist on escorting his stepson round his watering holes and exhibiting him proudly to his drinking partners: 'There he stands! Dan Leno! *My* boy! The most famous man on earth—and *I* trained him!' 'See that,' he'd exclaim, pointing to Dan's diamond ring, 'Things like that don't grow on gooseberry bushes, do they? Who is responsible for putting that ring on that finger? Ask the boy! He'll tell you! I am!'

Dan Leno's first London appearance as an adult was on 5 October 1885 at the Forester's Music Hall in Mile End. For a salary of £5 a week he gave his champion clog-dance and two comic songs. The clog-dance, to his amazement and dismay, died the proverbial death, but the songs were an immediate success. The clogs, so respected in the North, meant nothing in the South, but Dan began to discover that his songs had the potential of meaning something everywhere. The first he sang was called 'Going to Buy Milk for the Twins' and this he performed dressed as a down-trodden but still-spirited working-class woman, the sort that ought to have gone under but never did. The second was called 'When Rafferty Raffled His Watch', the chorus of which went like this:

The fender was chained to the fireplace;
   The poker was chained to the hob;
You bet your life, if they'd been loose,
   They'd both have been on the job.
The tables and chairs were tumbled downstairs;
   We'd plenty of Irish and Scotch;
And the divil's own row there was that night
   When Rafferty raffled his watch.

Later the same evening Dan also made his debut in the West End when he took the stage, with the same act, at the Middlesex Music Hall in Drury Lane. At the Old Mo, as the Middlesex was known having been built on the site of the old Mogul Tavern, the occasion was advertised, as it had been at the Forester's, as:

First Appearance in London of
DAN LENO,
The great Irish Comic Vocalist and present Champion Dancer of the World.

Dan shared the bill with the Matinetti Troupe who were giving their 'screaming eccentricity', an intentionally laughable melodrama called *A Terrible Night*, Fred Coyne 'the Sterling Comedian', Vernon Grey 'the Funny Ventriloquist', Harry White's Minstrels and a dozen other Old Mo regulars, and found that his songs fared as well, and his clog-dancing fared as badly, in the West End as both had done in the East End.

The hard commercial proof of Dan's success came when he was booked for a second week at the Middlesex and immediately billed as 'Another Middlesex Favourite—Don't Fail to See Him'. By the time he was retained for a third week he must have begun to believe his own billing:

The Talk of London
DAN LENO
Champion Dancer of the World and Funniest
of All Comic Vocalists

Indeed, he probably would have believed it had he not found himself appearing shortly after with another, equally unknown, comedian whose billing was even more magniloquent:

> 'The World-renowned, Funny, Comical, Laughable, and Original Side-splitting Comedian. The most Versatile Comedian we have at the present upon the Music-hall stage. Every song funny! Every song in character!! Every song copyright!!! Not one, but all!!! Come and have a laugh! Remember, this is the only one of his name in the Concert Hall.'

However believable or unbelievable his billing, Dan Leno's bookings were real enough. Soon he was appearing all over London—at Collins' Music Hall in Islington, at the Queen's in Poplar, at the Standard in Pimlico, at the Forester's, at the Old Mo—often appearing at three different halls in one evening. At the same time he was making sorties back into the provinces to fulfil old contracts and undertake new ones. He might not yet be 'The Talk of London', 'All the Rage' and 'Everybody's Favourite' as the posters proclaimed, but there was no doubt about it: Dan Leno had arrived to stay.

CHAPTER THREE

From the Old Mo to the Lane

Take a romantically farcical fairy tale, set it to music, people it with men dressed as women, women dressed as men, humans dressed as animals, lard it with spectacle and slapstick, topical gags and old chestnuts, community singing and audience participation, and you have that phenomenal phenomenon called British pantomime. It is a unique form of entertainment and for nearly two centuries now it has been the Englishman's favourite form of theatre. More people go to a pantomime than to any other kind of live show.

Traditional English pantomime owes a little to the Greeks and Romans, rather more to the Italian tradition of *commedia dell' arte* and French fairground entertainments, and a great deal to John Rich, the eighteenth-century harlequin, and Joseph Grimaldi, the nineteenth-century clown, for the first established pantomime in London and the second made it a national cult. But the pantomimes of Rich and Grimaldi were not pantomimes that we would recognise as such today. They were one-act entertainments, lasting perhaps two hours, and divided into roughly eighteen scenes. The 'opening', which was always the shorter part of the performance, was usually based on the story of a nursery rhyme or a classical myth, and invariably involved a pair of young lovers having to flee from the girl's disapproving father and unsuitable suitor. Just as things were getting really sticky for the young ones, a benevolent figure of the Fairy Godmother variety would take the stage, save the day and transform the characters from the opening into the characters of the harlequinade. The youth would become Harlequin—and, as often as not, be set a testing task to perform and be equipped with a magic stick or bat, with which to protect himself and perform outrageous tricks to the delight of the audience—and the girl would become the loyal Columbine. The hard-hearted father would become the Clown and the unsavoury suitor would probably be transformed into the Pantaloon—in which guise the older pair would continue to pursue the younger pair, getting involved in all sorts of scrapes and escapades on the way. But whatever happened by way of slapstick lunacy during the harlequinade, one thing was certain: in the end good triumphed over evil and the young lovers lived happily ever after.

By the time Dan Leno came to star in pantomime the harlequinade that had been at the very heart of 'panto' had become a mere postscript and the fairy-tale opening had been expanded and elaborated and had become almost the whole show. Modern British pantomime resembles late-Victorian pantomime much more closely than late-Victorian pantomime resembled Regency pantomime. Sentimentalists today, firmly believing that nowadays even nostalgia isn't what it used to be, bemoan the decline of pantomime and complain that, where once pantomime swept you away into a magical world of make-believe, the modern 'panto' gives you little more than a vulgar television spectacular in pantomime costume. Of course, there are differences between the pantomimes of today and a century ago—they were much longer then, more spectacular, often written in rhyming couplets, and owed nothing to television, though much to the music hall—but at the Palladium in the 1970s and Drury Lane in the 1890s you would have seen Christmas entertainments that were clearly very close cousins, if not precisely twins.

The Argyle Theatre of Varieties in Argyle Street in Birkenhead opened on 21 December 1868 and, if Birkenhead folklore is to be believed, one of the leading lights of the production was young Dan Patrick, aged eight years and one day, making his pantomime debut with the rest of the Leno troupe. If this was his first appearance in the form of theatre that he was one day destined to make all his own, it was an inauspicious start: the profit for the pantomime's first week was eleven pence.

The man really responsible for launching Leno into pantomime was George Conquest, one of the nineteenth century's most influential men of the theatre, who took over the Surrey Theatre in Blackfriars Road in 1881 and made it famous for its melodramas and pantomimes, many of which he wrote, produced, painted the scenery for and played in himself. He was known as a master of flying ballets and every kind of acrobatic effect (in one pantomime thirty different trapdoors were brought into play), teased as an actor who had an impossible stammer off-stage that never troubled him on stage, and acknowledged as an impresario with an uncanny knack for spotting new talent. He spotted Dan singing 'Going to Buy Milk for the Twins' at the Old Mo, saw how well the skirts became him and booked him to play Jack's mother in his production of *Jack and the Beanstalk* for Christmas 1886. Lydia Reynolds was also engaged to play Mercury and they received a joint salary of £20 per week.

The company was a strong one (as well as Dan and Lydia, it included Johnny Danvers, Maud Stafford, Lillie Ernest, the Sisters Watson, and Tom Costello playing the inexplicable role of Mephistopheles Muldoon) and the pantomime was a success, notably so for Dan who collected good notices—'A more amusing Dame Durden than Mr. Dan Leno it would not be easy to discover', the *Era*—and a request from Mr. Conquest on only the second night of the pantomime's run that Dan should come back next year as principal comedian, with Lydia as principal boy.

Sinbad and the Little Old Man of the Sea, Or, The Tinker, The Tailor, The Soldier, The Sailor, Apothecary, Ploughboy, Gentleman Thief, was the improbable title of the Surrey's pantomime in 1887 and Dan was a suitably eccentric Tinpanz the Tinker. The *Era* described him as 'a capital tinker, full of drollery and grotesque business . . . most humorous throughout the pantomine' and the *Stage* applauded his 'dry genuine humour . . . every movement is a signal for laughter and his dance on the rolling vessel is a sight to see.'

Fortunately for Dan, it was a sight seen by Augustus Harris, the most important theatrical manager in the country, and the producer of the pantomimes at the capital's premier playhouse, the Theatre Royal in Drury Lane. When Dan first came to London without his parents, Johnny Danvers had taken him to see 'The Lane' for the first time. Dan had walked up the steps and knelt on the topmost one, and said 'Johnny, I shall act here some day!'

The day turned out to be 26 December 1888. The pantomime

was *Babes in the Wood* and the stars: Harry Nicholls and Herbert Campbell as a pair of obese Babes and Harriet Vernon, one of the most substantial and popular Principal Boys of her day, as a voluptuous Robin Hood. Lydia Reynolds, although offered a part, did not appear, having retired from the stage into permanent domesticity to have the second of her and Dan's six children. Dan played the Baroness and impressed the public and his employer sufficiently for Harris to book him immediately for the next three pantomimes. Harris then booked him for a further five years. Eventually, as Dan used to boast, he was booked 'for the term of my natural life'.

Augustus Harris's pantomimes were noted for their scenic splendour and extravagance. There were at least fifteen elaborate scenes, a cast of over a hundred, ballets, choirs, acrobats, marionettes, processions, animals *and* a harlequinade, for although Harris was often accused of vulgarising the pantomime by placing so much emphasis on lavish spectacle, and of destroying the old traditions by importing music hall artistes to play the leading parts, he had a soft spot for the harlequinade and the entertainment never concluded without a brief romp with Harlequin and Columbine, Clown and Pantaloon. For the first month of the run the pantomime would be performed twice daily, at 1.30 p.m. and at 6.30 p.m., and would invariably last for over four hours. The public obviously liked what it was offered: the 1888 production of *Babes in the Wood* did not close until 27 April 1889.

As the Baroness in *Babes in the Wood* Dan had not had a great deal to do. As Mrs. Simpson, Jack's elderly and downtrodden mother, in *Jack and the Beanstalk* in 1889 he was given more scope, scoring particularly with his dances ('they are electrical') and a supposedly serious ballad that he was quite unable to get through because of the chorus of cats and other farmyard animals coming from Mrs. Simpson's back yard:

> Our mother Nature seems to seek
> A well-earned rest at close of day!
> Her task is done; and (so to speak)
> She's 'washed-up' and she's 'cleared away!'

And, like a good dame, always will
  At eventide with cosy chat
With her sweet voice the silence fill
  With sounds of peace (CAT outside 'Miow!')
                There's a cat

Ah me! what lessons can we learn!
  If we but hearken to her—(Miow!)
On all sides—ev'ry way we turn
  She'll teach us (Miow!) Oh! stop that
By rippling stream—through wood and dell
  In peaceful vale—on mountain brow;
You hear her (Miow?) I mean—(Miow!) well
  I think I'll give it up! (Miow! Miow!)

The number was written by Harry Nicholls, who as well as being the Lane's principal comedian in the 'eighties wrote or collaborated on the book of most of the pantomimes. The rhyming and the rhythm of the writing were kept to a formula and the more predictable and familiar it all was the more the public felt happy and at home. Here is Jack, played by Harriet Vernon, breaking some bad news to his mother in a piece of dialogue that audiences at the Lane in 1889 knew was corny but found irresistible:

JACK [*outside*]: Mother! Mother!
MRS. S. Ah! here he is!
  [*enter* JACK *enthusiastically*]
JACK: See, Ma, what I have got!
MRS. S: Something to eat, my dear?
JACK: No!
MRS. S: I thought not!
JACK: [*aside*]: I wonder if there's going to be a row?
MRS. S [*crying*]: I can't go on much longer—[*suddenly*] Where's the cow?
JACK: [*aside*]: Now for it! [*aloud*] Ma dear, it is gone!
MRS. S [*shrieking*]: What, dead!
JACK: No!

MRS. S [*seizing him*]: Give it me! Or else I'll punch your head! Give me my cow!

[*searching in his pockets*] Or let me know the worst!

JACK: I've sold it!

MRS. S [*calming down*]: Then, why not say so at first?

JACK: You wouldn't give me time!

MRS. S: What did he fetch?

JACK [*nervously*]: No money!

MRS. S [*alarmed*]: No? What then?

JACK: These beans!

MRS. S [*after a pause of utter astonishment, goes for him*]: You wretch!

JACK [*dodging her*] Now, keep away, Ma!

MRS. S: Come here!

JACK: No, I shan't!

MRS. S: I'll flay you, when I get at you!

JACK: You can't,

Now, pray be calm, and hear what I've to say,
These beans will make my fortune some fine day.

MRS. S: [*dubiously*]: Oh! How?

JACK: Because they're magic.

MRS. S: Here's a treat!

Then some day, we may something have to eat?
My present pangs of hunger 'twill assuage
To think I'll have a meal in my old age!

One day in 1890 Harris came up with the notion of allowing Dan to put away his skirts.

'Dan, how do you think you'd be as a man?' he asked.

'Well, I don't know,' said Dan, 'But I think I *ought* to be all right; because, you see, I was born that way.'

So it came to pass in *Beauty and the Beast* that Dan played Mr. Lombarde Streete, a City merchant and father of Beauty (played by Belle Bilton, who was then Lady Dunlo and later became Countess of Clancarty), with Vesta Tilley, the greatest of all male impersonators, as Principal Boy, and the two stout funny-men, Harry Nicholls and Herbert Campbell, as the Merchant's Elderly Daughters.

Beauty and the Beast was Harry Nicholls' last pantomime at the Lane. He and Campbell had been hardy annuals there for eight years, so that the end of their partnership was a matter for real regret among the 'panto' regulars in the audience, but regret quickly turned into gratitude when the audiences discovered that the splendid team of Nicholls and Campbell was to be replaced by the even more rewarding team of Campbell and Leno. 'What a pair, inimitable in everything they did,' was the verdict of Jimmy Glover, for many years the resident musical director at the Lane who must have seen them in action as often as anyone. 'They worked hand-in-hand for the joke, the laugh, the success. Separated in two different *métiers* in the music hall for nine months of the year, each in turn made notes and when they finally met compared, amalgamated and joined the parts together.'

Max Beerbohm, when asked by foreign visitors to show them something inherently British would take them first to Westminster Abbey and the Tower of London, and then to a music hall to see Herbert Campbell. He was a mountain of man, a jolly John Bull with bluff manner and booming voice to match. Born in 1846, he had started as part of a nigger minstrel troupe, but went on to become one of the most popular comedians on the halls, specialising in fairly heavy-handed parodies and songs and gags that were broad rather than blue. Weighing in at nineteen stone, he was the perfect contrast to the nimble little Leno and when they came on in *Humpty Dumpty* in 1891 to play the first of their famous 'double scenes' together, it was clear to all at once that here was a marriage that had been made in heaven. Campbell played a tremulous King of Hearts, with Dan as his not-very-doting spouse:

KING [*shouting*]: I want my breakfast! [*lingering over property ham*] That ham I don't dare cut. Whatever shall I do?

[*The* QUEEN *suddenly appears at door*]

QUEEN: Why, get your hair cut!

KING: My swe-et one!

QUEEN [*stalking to chair, very disagreeable*]: Well, my pretty?

KING [*aside*]: That sounds bad. [*aloud*]: Have you had a good night's rest, love?

QUEEN [*icily*]: If I had,
Or if I hadn't, you would care a lot!
[*whimpering*] You won't care much if I died!
KING [*aside*]: Well—er—p'raps not!
QUEEN [*sharply*]: What's that?
KING: I said how hot this tea is, dear. [*trying to soothe her makes things worse*] Though it's been standing some time.
QUEEN: Now, look here, if you've made up your mind to have a row—
KING [*aghast*]: I! Scotland Yard! what have I done wrong now?
QUEEN: Oh, raise your voice before the servants, do!
KING [*trying to be calm, whispers in rage*]: I haven't raised it yet—
QUEEN: Yes, that's like you.
Hiss at me all the insults that you can—
Because you dare not speak out like a man.
KING: I shall go raving mad!
QUEEN: Come, that is news.
KING: My bitter . . .
QUEEN: Now your own sweet language use.
[*During all this a* FLUNKY *has been serving the breakfast—not taking the very smallest notice of the row*].
Why don't you strike me next?
KING [*savagely seizing ham*]: I wish I could! I will strike something though.
[*Knocks the ham about the head of the* FLUNKY *and sinks exhausted in chair*] That's done me good!
[*The* FLUNKY *picks up the ham—wipes it with serviette, and places it without the slightest emotion on the table*]
And now let's have some breakfast, what d'ye say?
QUEEN: I have no appetite—[*to* FLUNKIES] So clear away.

Also in the cast of *Humpty Dumpty* that year were Little Tich, who abandoned his famous music hall boots, which were literally as long as he was tall, to play the title part, and a twenty-one-year-old Marie Lloyd, as Princess Allfair, who though not yet the undisputed Queen of the Music Hall, was already gaining the reputation for sauciness that was later to make her so notorious and so popular. Said the *Daily Telegraph*, 'Miss Marie Lloyd as the Princess Allfair was prettily coquettish and made on the whole the sprightliest of heroines, but some of her attitudes need a little more toning down and are unsuitable to the medium of Drury Lane, which is bound to maintain a certain dignity even in its liveliest moments.'

In *Little Bo Peep* in 1892 Herbert and Dan swapped sexes, Dan appearing as Daddy Thumb, 'a woodcutter who at the first sign of danger cuts his own stick', and Herbert as his wife, 'a Goody who doesn't moderate the rancour of her tongue'. Little Tich played Hop O' My Thumb, their youngest, and Marie Lloyd played a Little Red Riding Hood who was not as demure as some of her audience might have expected and hoped. In one scene she got out of bed and started searching underneath it for a chamber-pot! The following year she made her last appearance in pantomime at Drury Lane, as Polly Perkins in *Robinson Crusoe*, with Little Tich as Man Friday, and Dan as a Mrs. Crusoe half-crazed with love for the piratical Will Atkins of Herbert Campbell. If it was not Augustus Harris's most critically acclaimed production, it was certainly one of his most spectacular, climaxing with 'The History of England in Twenty Minutes: A Grand Procession of the Kings and Queens of England from William I to Her Imperial Majesty Queen Victoria'!

In 1894 Herbert played Alice the Cook and Dan played Idle Jack in *Dick Whittington*. The moment that appealed most to audience and critics was when an increasingly manic Jack, waiting, intoxicated and impatient, outside the village church for his bride-to-be, having soliloquised a piece of appalling doggerel, turned on the church's deaf verger with a parody of R. G. Knowles, the self-styled 'Very Peculiar American Comedian', who was currently much in vogue having broken all records at the Empire, Leicester Square, by remaining on the bill for seventy-three consecutive weeks, so proving that Dan was not only a dancer, singer and comic, but also a gifted impressionist as well:

JACK: At last this is my happy wedding morn,
And I've had to put my hat on with a shoe-horn.

And I'm to be Queen of the May, mother, I'm to be Queen of the May,
The may, the might, the shall, the will love, honour, and obey;
That simile is rather mixed, I think,
And so I rather think was last night's drink.
Somehow this morning I can't think a think.
Was Pa-as-is-to-be also as drunk?
Did he at dawn, like me, feel quite unable
To hunt the pink rats off his dressing table?
Did alligators climb the window blinds?
Did bright green kangaroos of various kinds
Sing comic choruses all round his bed?
Did both his eyeballs feel like molten lead?
Had he a tongue that felt like wool and glue?
Did nervous twitchings shake him through and through?
Did he know what he wanted to take most?
The Pledge, or a B. and S. and some dry toast?
A B. and S.—soda and lots of brandy!
I wonder if a public-house is handy?
No. There's a procession coming up the hill.
I wish I didn't feel so beastly ill!
In yonder chariot do I see my bride.
Or is't a Hampstead tramcar full inside?
It stops by yonder pump. It is the milk!
(Curious that nothing rhymes to milk but Bilk).

[*Bells stop ringing*]

The bells have stopped. The organ, too, that's rum.
Why—why the Dickens doesn't Alice come?

[*To Old Man*]

I say, are you the Sexton?

O.M.: No, Sir, I'm the Verger.

JACK: Where do you verge? I mean, look here—you know—I'm going to be married [*drops into an imitation of R. G. Knowles*], and my wife—that is, my wife that is to be—is rather late. I don't think she can have forgotten altogether, though it may have slipped her memory, till she took the cake—that is, the wedding-that-is-to-be-cake—with the milk. I don't mean the cake is going to marry the milk; but she took the cake and the milk for the wedding; I don't mean she mistook them—the cake and the milk, for a wedding—but being a Miss she took the cake and the milk in the morning. I don't mean the Miss took the cake and the milk mixed, but took them separately in the morning, and put them down together, in the—cupboard; she said, 'Oh my! bless me, of course I knew there was something I'd forgotten. I must go right up the stairs and put on my nice new lace-trimmed bonnet, with fruit and flowers on it, because I have just got to run up to Highgate and get married. And there is that poor, dear young man of mine standing outside the church now, and if I don't get there right soon he'll be so disappointed.'

Ha! Ha!
Ho! Ho!
He'll look to the East, and he'll look to the West,
But he will not see a wedding!

O.M.: I'm a little 'ard o' 'earing, Sir. Would you mind saying all that over again?

In 1895, Dan played the Baroness, and Herbert the Baron in *Cinderella*—the title part being taken by Isa Bowman who, incidentally, had once been one of Lewis Carroll's 'child friends',—and the sort of material they used and the way they must have put it across is well illustrated by the scene in which the Baroness turns on her unfortunate second husband and does her best to blacken his reputation in front of her devoted daughters (Ugly Sisters, played on this occasion, by ladies). The scene, cluttered with old chestnuts and topical allusions, has Dan throwing himself about the stage with abandon, rattling off his lines at speed, with Herbert stolidly booming out his short, sharp rejoinders and asides. It's typical:

BARONESS [*drying her eyes*]: And now, on the anniversary of our wedding day, he knocks my children about and abuses me. Ah! well, he'll find out what he's lost when he loses me!

BARON [*aside—in rapture*]: Lose her! [*sadly*] No, 'tis but a dream.
BARONESS: Oh! That my first husband was alive!
BARON: Would that he were!
BARONESS: My first husband was the father of those girls, and do you know what he did?
BARON: He died, and I don't blame him.

[*The* THREE WOMEN *stand over him threateningly.*]

BARON [*weakly*]: My dear, I didn't speak.
BARONESS: Don't dear me, sir. Ah! what a fool I was to be led away by his words. He promised to give me a happy home and I—poor simple child—believed him. Look at the position I threw up for a thing like that.
BARON: You know you were only a barmaid at the 'Pig and Whistle'—and as to your two girls—
BARONESS [*dramatically*]: Stay! Strike me, if you will, but spare Oh! spare—my babes.

[*She tenderly leads her children off, saying,*]

Go! my poor dears—and mourn your mother's lot.
CLOR: Give him beans, mamma!
ANG: Let him have it hot!

[*Exeunt* CLORINDA *and* ANGELINA)

BARON [*with fear again*]: Well, my love—you know, after all, you were a barmaid.
BARONESS: That's right. Throw the bar in my face. And what if I was a barmaid? I flatter myself there were few like me.
BARON: None, my dear, none.
BARONESS: People used to come from miles round to see me. Why, I made the name of the place.
BARON: So you did—my dear—so you did. It got the name of the 'Old Curiosity Shop'.
BARONESS: Oh, indeed! Then if I am a curiosity, why did you marry me?
BARON: I was led to believe you had charge of the till.
BARONESS: Well, come to that, I didn't marry you for your

beauty alone. No, I hoped to marry my daughters through you. I sacrificed myself for nothing. They are still single.

BARON: There, there. Don't be alarmed! There is yet time. Somebody must marry them.

BARONESS: Oh, I shouldn't bestow them on any Tom, Dick or Harry. My idea is a Lord or Duke, or even a millionaire.

BARON: I know that millionaire! He comes from Africa.

BARONESS: And goes into Society. All Rhodes lead to Earls—if not to Court.

BARON: Your girls may pick some husband up at the party we are giving tomorrow.

BARONESS: Party! A nice party it'll be, I expect. We're simply ruined.

BARON: Your fault, my love. You would buy those dresses.

BARONESS: It was Drury Lane that drove me to it. Since I saw those lovely dresses in 'Cheer, Boys, Cheer!' I have felt bound to have the same. And they would have been cheap if the dear girls had 'gone off' through their aid—

BARON [*aside*]: They would have had to meet men who had 'gone off' first.

BARONESS: They're living images of their mother.

BARON: That's what I complain of.

Sir Augustus Harris—he was knighted in 1891, not for his services to pantomime but because he happened to be Sheriff of the City of London when the German Emperor paid an official visit—died in the summer of 1896, but the tradition he had established as 'Druriolanus' was continued and built upon by Arthur Collins, his right-hand man, who succeeded him as Lessee and Manager at the Lane. On the whole the *Aladdin* of 1896 was not considered a great success, though Jimmy Glover recalled some lovely moments ('The Widow Twankey when wealthy shovelling sovereigns out of a coal scuttle, Leno and Campbell in a balloon surveying London with caustic comment, hanging a spirit stove over the side to cook a bloater for breakfast and to boil a kettle in mid-air—the jerk of the airship, the loss of the bloater, the sudden interjection of Herbert Campbell, "Why, blimey, there's a man picking up our bloater in Cheapside and he's eating it too."") and Dan's Widow Twankey picked up some enthusiastic notices. 'Singing, dancing or acting Mr. Leno is at his best this season', said the *Stage*. 'His acting . . . has vastly improved: there is more continuity; it is more consistent. In this way the comedian gains; he stands out through the production as certainly the most clever actor who has been seen for many years in this class of work.'

Many judged this to be Dan's most complete Dame, the working-class washerwoman whose life is a triumphant series of disasters, the full awfulness of which she never appreciates, so accustomed is she to the inevitability of being one of life's losers:

> Oh dear! What is there about washing that makes people so bad-tempered? I'm sorry I ever adopted it as a profession. But there, when Mustapha left me to battle with an untrusting world what could I do? I tried lady barbering, but the customers were too attentive and I—poor simple child—was full of unsophisticatedness and I believed their honeyed words. I remember young Lord Plumpler agitated me so with his badinage that there was a slight accident. I believe he would have proposed to me, but in my confusion I cut the end of his nose off. Ah! it was a near shave.
>
> Then I went on the stage as Juliet. Oh, the bouquets they threw at me! Not silly useless hot-house flowers, but cauliflowers and garden fruit like that. When they repaired the theatre I asked for a re-engagement, but the manager was out. Then I had an idea. All Society ladies were learning to be useful in dressmaking, millinery, painting and journalism. So I founded this select laundry for the daughters of decayed noblemen. It was all right at first, but I soon found that as my pupils left me my trade decreased—every lady became her own laundress. Never mind; the weather forecast says it will rain in Brixton, so there may be a storm in Hackney. Then, if it rains, we shall have water and business will look up.

Dan's tenth pantomime at Drury Lane was, as his first had been, *Babes in the Wood*, and if Jimmy Glover is to be believed, the combination of Campbell and Leno as Chrissie and Reggie was even more memorable than Campbell and Nicholls as Bertie and Cissy had been a decade before: 'one a little, lean, slippery, electric, never-at-rest spark; the other a great, big avoirdupois, prosperous-looking Babe of twenty stone, falling to sleep when they are lost in the woods and, before so doing, singing, of all things, the angel's hymn from *Hansel and Gretel* quite seriously to a dumb-struck house.'

Johnny Danvers, Dan's contemporaneous uncle and lifelong friend, was recruited to play Ali Baba in *The Forty Thieves* in 1898 and, having become something of a music hall favourite himself—he was for twenty years one of the leading 'Mohawk Minstrels' and his playing of the tambourine was unrivalled!—he now became something of a Drury Lane stalwart as well. He and Herbert were Dan's closest friends (he named his first and fourth sons after them) and neither of them ever showed any jealousy or resentment towards Dan, whose popularity had by now far outstripped theirs. A Drury Lane pantomime without Dan Leno had become as unthinkable as Christmas without Santa Claus. The audience adored him whether he appeared as a man (as he did as Abdullah in *The Forty Thieves*) or as a woman. Indeed the cheers that greeted him as Dame Trot in *Jack and the Beanstalk* in 1899 were written in to the script, so predictable were they:

ALL: She comes! she comes! the Dame appears!
Hurrah! hurrah! We hope she hears.
[*Enter Dame* TROT, *who comes down.*]

CHORUS.
Behold this must be Dan!
DAME: Oh, look at my fascinating stare;
Oh, look at my smile so very fair!
ALL: So beat him if you can,
He's a popular com-e-di-an.
Hurrah!

In *Sleeping Beauty and the Beast* in 1900 Leno and Campbell, as Queen Ravia and King Screwdolph, received the ultimate accolade: an ovation from an audience that hadn't even seen their faces! In the second scene of the 'panto', four attendants came onto the stage bearing two curtained palanquins, from the inside of one of which Herbert's voice was heard inquiring, 'Have you anything to do this afternoon, my dear?' From inside the other Dan replied 'No, I've nothing on!' The audience roared and the roars reached a crescendo as the flunkeys bore off the palanquins, the bottoms of which then fell out to reveal four utterly unmistakable feet. To enter and exit unseen and yet have the audience in your thrall is an achievement few could encompass.

Sleeping Beauty and the Beast was the first of more than a dozen Drury Lane pantomimes written by J. Hickory Wood. He abandoned most of the traditional rhyming couplets and produced scripts that were robust, more modern and more obviously 'funny' than those of his predecessors at the Lane. They continued to be used all over the country for many years after his death in 1913, and there are still one or two theatres in the 1970s that base their Christmas pantomime on a 'Hickory Wood original'. His second 'panto' for the Lane was *Bluebeard*, in which Dan played a Sister Anne who simply could not get Herbert Campbell's Bluebeard to fall in love with her:

> Men don't easily fall in love with me—not suddenly. I sort of grow on them. Then they fall quite gracefully in love with me. But once they're there they're there for ever. I'm a sort of female rattlesnake. I weave spells round them. I'm one of those —you know—those foghorns you hear on the river. I don't mean foghorns but you know—tut, tut, sirens, that's it—I'm a siren.

Hickory Wood managed better than anyone to write lines that perfectly suited the contrasting styles of Leno and Campbell. Here is a scene from *Bluebeard* where the comical couple are thumbing through Bradshaw. It is a piece of inspired nonsense that delighted audiences at the turn of the century and still manages to raise a smile:

ANNE: Where are you going?
BLUEBEARD: I'm going to a place called Puzzleton.

ANNE: Puzzleton? How do you get there?

BLUEBEARD: That's what I'm trying to find out. Here you are. There's a train at 9.40 marked B. What does that mean?

ANNE: B? Cattle only.

BLUEBEARD: That's no good.

ANNE: There's one at 10.30 marked J. See what J means.

BLUEBEARD: J—see page 406.

ANNE: There it is—'J—see page 108.'

BLUEBEARD: Why, that's where we started from.

ANNE: So it is. What silly things guides are.

BLUEBEARD: Here you are, J—I've got it, 10.30 train to Puzzleton. 'This train runs on Sundays, Wednesdays and Fridays only during September and July, except on the 15th of each month, then it runs on Tuesday and Thursday and Saturday from the 9th of June to the 8th of August, except on Bank holidays and Sundays, when it starts at 6.50. On all other occasions it runs as usual.'

ANNE: That's a very good train.

BLUEBEARD: Yes, but I don't think I'll go by it.

ANNE: Let me see. I understand these things. Look here! You start by the 11.30 express; that takes you to the edge of the desert in time to catch the 2.30 camel; the camel brings you across the desert to Tra-ra-ra Junction, where you meet the 5.16 elephant that brings you to the 9.20 steamer.

BLUEBEARD: That isn't a steamer; it's a balloon.

ANNE: So it is. Well! The 9.20 balloon brings you as far as Muddle Circus, where you take the blue bus with the umbrella over the driver. See? Look for yourself.

BLUEBEARD: 11.30 express. Here we are. Z—what's that? Z—Shrove Tuesday and Christmas Day only.

Mother Goose in 1902 was generally regarded as Hickory Wood's best script—he created the pantomime story that everyone now accepts as being as old as the Cinderella legend—and Dan's portrayal of the title part regarded as his finest pantomime performance. His entrance, devised by Arthur Collins, never failed to bring the house down. He came on riding a little country cart pulled by donkeys, only to be met and overturned by a speedy motorcar. Amid all the confusion, with Leno helping the donkeys to their feet, chasing after the geese that had been perched in the cart, running hither and thither, he turned on the car owners:

MOTHER GOOSE: Oh! If I could get at your eyes, I'd scratch them out! Yes! You do well to cover yourselves all over with scrap iron when you rush about the country like this! Come out of your meat-hasteners and talk to me, if you dare. Oh! I forgot! They're sure to be foreigners! Vour avez smashe mon carri-age, and I demande le damage—see? It's very evident they're not French! Itsen das cartsen splitsen—donner und blitzen! So! And they're not Germans either. Senors! El Carto pieceo Broko! El demando Compensationo! Caramba! Caraggio! Caracas Cocoa! Well! I don't believe they know any language!

FIRST MOTORMAN: Why cawn't you talk English?

MOTHER GOOSE: That sounds a familiar accent.

FIRST MOTORMAN: We ain't no foreigners! I druv a Brixton 'bus for twenty years.

SECOND MOTORMAN: Yuss! And mine was a privileged keb in Euston station.

MOTHER GOOSE: And I've been wasting my education over them like this! Police!

While Hickory Wood provided a basic script as the foundation of the show, Arthur Collins, Dan and Herbert then built on it, adding to it, thinking of fresh business, introducing various props, improvising gags, making suggestions. Hickory Wood attended the rehearsals and recorded a few moments of one of them. It gives an engaging insight into the way in which the artistes and the director slowly built up the performance.

HERBERT [*stolidly*]: I say, mother, you are a swell!

DAN [*wearily*]: Do you think I look expensive enough?

HERBERT: Rather! You look like a walking Bank of England.

DAN: Of course, in my position I want to look wealthy.
HERBERT: Yes! That dress must have cost a lot of eggs.
DAN: I don't care, but I do grudge having so many expensive things underneath I daren't show—[*to Collins*] I say, Arthur, suppose Comelli designs these expensive things for me.
COLLINS: Well, I don't know, Dan. We can't afford to pay Comelli his price for designing things you daren't show.
DAN [*with a twinkle in his eye*]: Yes! But you might have a line in the programme to say that, as these things were executed by Alias from Comelli's designs the management had decided they were too good to waste, so—
HERBERT [*strictly on business*]: Come on, Dan, let's get on with it. Play the game.
DAN: All right! All right! [*refers to part*] Let me see. What do I say now?
HERBERT [*severely*]: You don't say anything at all. It's me. [*reads*] It's the same with me. I've got sealskin socks on this very minute.
DAN: I'm sure we all ought to marry into the aristocracy, you and Jill and I.
HERBERT: What? You get married? [*with intense solemnity*] Ha, ha, ha! [*to Dan who has paused*] Go on. It's your turn.
DAN: I'm waiting for my cue!
HERBERT: Well, I gave you your cue!
DAN: No, you didn't! My cue is—'Jack laughs.'
HERBERT: Well, I did laugh! [*to Collins*] Didn't I?
COLLINS: Yes, Dan. It's all right. He laughed!
DAN [*innocently surprised*]: Was that a laugh? I thought he had the croup. [*refers to part*] Why not? I've been married, haven't I?
HERBERT: Yes; but that was to father—not to a stranger—
DAN [*aside*]: I've heard that one before.
COLLINS [*to rest of company, whose conversation has gradually risen to flood-tide*]: Will you ladies and gentlemen please be quiet? We can't hear a word we're saying here.
HERBERT [*resuming*]: I'm going to marry Gretchen.
DAN [*turning over 'galley-pulls' and getting somewhat entangled therein*]: Well, that's what I came here to do. I've no particular

reason for doing anything or being anywhere. I'm really going somewhere else. Come, Priscilla! [*surprised*] That's funny! I appear to go off here with a goose! When did the goose come on?

HERBERT [*judicially*]: There's something wrong: my next speech doesn't fit in.

COLLINS [*coming to the rescue*]: Let me see. What page are you on, then?

DAN: Page nine!

COLLINS: Oh, you've turned over two pages! [*puts things straight*] Now you're all right. Go ahead!

DAN: Oh, by-the-by, Jack, I've been buying some ancestors.

HERBERT: What are ancestors?

DAN: Don't you know? They're relations who grow on a family tree.

HERBERT: What kind of a tree is that?

DAN: It's a—[*drops 'galley-pull' and picks it up again*] Yes, it's true! I am beautiful! I'm—[*stops abruptly*] That sounds silly.

COLLINS [*again coming to the rescue*]: You've got on the wrong page again, Dan [*rearranges*] There you are! Go on!

HERBERT [*meditatively*]: You know I fancy this scene is going to turn out very funny.

DAN: Yes, I can see a lot in it. [*resumes*] A family tree is a kind of —sort of a—Give me a piece of chalk!

HERBERT: Here you are! [*tentatively to Collins*] I suppose this is where I give Dan the chalk?

COLLINS: That's right.

DAN: This is the tree; this is the trunk, and—[*pauses*] What do I do with the chalk?

COLLINS: Oh! There'll be pictures on the stage, and you'll turn one round and draw on the back of it.

DAN [*relieved*]: I see! [*resumes*] These are the branches, and these are the tree-roots that—[*crawling on hands and knees down stage, chalking and improvising as he crawls*]—the tree-roots that go right away down into the main sewer.

COLLINS [*to prompter*]: Put that down!

HERBERT: Right! [*to Dan*] And when I say 'parsley-bed', you put your foot through the picture and everybody comes on. [*to Collins, encouragingly*] That'll be all right, governor!

DAN [*agreeing*]: Yes; I can see a lot of fun in that scene.

COLLINS: All right! [*to rest of company*] Come along, ladies and gentlemen, picture scene over, everybody on!

Charlie Chaplin described Dan as 'the greatest comedian since the legendary Grimaldi' and, certainly, Grimaldi and Leno have long been accepted as the two giants of pantomime. But Dan in pantomime was not universally acclaimed. When William Archer, the Australian-born critic who was responsible for bringing Ibsen before the British public, witnessed *Humpty Dumpty* at the Lane in 1891 he was not impressed. 'When Mr. Dan Leno exhibited himself in red flannel petticoat and pair of stays, the whole house literally yelled with delight,' he told his readers. 'I don't seem to yearn for the privilege . . . of admiring Mr. Dan Leno in deshabille; but amid all that vast audience, I was evidently in a minority of one.'

Actually, it was a minority of two. That other noted Ibsenite, Bernard Shaw, found the antics at Drury Lane equally distressing:

> I hope I never again have to endure anything more dismally futile than the efforts of Mr. Leno and Mr. Herbert Campbell to start a passable joke in the course of their stumblings and wanderings through barren acres of gag on Boxing Night. Their attempts at a travesty of *Hamlet* reached a pitch of abject resourcelessness which could not have been surpassed if they had been a couple of school children called on for a prize-day Shakespearian recitation without any previous warning . . . If Mr. Dan Leno had asked for a hundred guinea tunic to wear during a single walk across the stage, no doubt he would have got it, with a fifty guinea hat and sword-belt to boot. If he had asked for ten guineas' worth of a competent dramatic humourist to provide him with at least one line that might not have been pirated from the nearest Cheap Jack, he would I suspect, have been asked whether he wished to make Drury Lane bankrupt.

CHAPTER FOUR

You must *know Mrs. Kelly!*

'Ever seen his eyes?' asked Marie Lloyd after Dan had died. 'The saddest eyes in the whole world. That's why we all laughed at Danny. Because if we hadn't laughed, we should have cried ourselves sick. I believe that's what real comedy is, you know. It's almost like crying.'

No one who saw Leno can have failed to notice those strange, enquiring eyes, dark and deeply sunken, 'wistful little black lamps' Seymour Hicks called them. They seemed the embodiment of all that was melancholy and yet managed to twinkle at the same time. They appeared to be gazing out into some other world beyond, yet simultaneously contrived to be darting looks all over the stage and auditorium, beadily observing every aspect of the here and now. His eyebrows were arched and quizzical and helped create the overall impression of distressed surprise that characterised the face.

The nose was slightly upturned with large nostrils. The ears were big too. The mouth was enormous. The lips were thin, but the mouth itself stretched right across his face and then dipped down at the edges. There was a dimple in his chin, a furrow between his eyebrows and a deep diagonal furrow coming from above each nostril down across the lower part of his cheeks. The eyebrows, the mouth, the dimple and the furrows he accentuated with his make-up, but off-stage or on he managed to look like a mystified marmoset unable to decide whether life was miserable or amusing, so settling for a mixture of both.

He was only five foot three, with a frail frame and hyperactive feet. Agile, light, ever scampering, far from there being any economy in his movements, he was perpetually wound up and always on the go. His body was as anxiously eager and as eagerly anxious as his face.

His voice had a strained quality to it too. It was quite light, rather thin, even a little husky, but with a wide-mouthed, tight-throated resonance, it had no difficulty filling the vast auditorium at Drury Lane or getting across the hubbub of the halls. He did not speak the Queen's English, but nor did he have a definite accent. There was an unmistakable Irish lilt to his voice—which combined with his early billing, led many to believe he was an Irishman—but, no doubt because of his years touring the North as a child, it had a certain North Country flavour to it as well. He often forgot his aitches and his gees—saying 'avin' and 'opin' and 'ikin'—and his 'ow' sounds would certainly have given Henry Higgins a turn, but as a whole his intonation reflected the received English of the Victorian lower middle class rather than the characteristic twang of the working class from any particular part of the country.

Although Dan Leno may not have had an obvious working-class accent, the personality he presented and the characters he created came, very obviously, from the same world as his audience. The music halls were the pleasure palaces of the people and Dan, like so many of the great stars of the music hall—Marie Lloyd, Albert Chevalier, George Robey, to name three whose names still mean something to us now—personified their daydreams and their deprivations. He was of the people and they knew it. His characters were larger than life, to be sure, and the mishaps that befell them often fantastic to the degree of absurdity, but they were all rooted in a hard reality that was totally recognisable to his public. He was an intensely *human* performer, but his humanity had nothing airy-fairy about it. He was down-to-earth, but, unlike so many other of the turns on the halls, never dirty. He cut straight to the bone, without ever going near the knuckle. No one ever accused Dan Leno of vulgarity. (While it was quite unthinkable that Marie Lloyd should have been included in the first Royal Command Performance at the Palace Theatre in 1912, Dan Leno was a perfectly acceptable dish to set before Queen Victoria twenty years before.) He created unique individuals, but they were individuals that sprang from the mass. He was never remote. However fantastic the character he played, however unlikely the tale he told, he remained totally real.

He was fully aware of what he was doing. 'The characters of my songs' he used to say, 'are all *founded on fact*'. He called them 'songs', but, in truth, they were not really songs at all. They were extraordinary monologues with a snatch of song at top and tail. When he first began to play the halls in London, he danced his clog-dance and sang more or less conventional comic songs in a more or less conventional way. But he quickly hung up his clogs and began to use the songs merely as pegs for his patter. And by the time he had reached the height of his fame and popularity, he had so perfected his style and honed it down to essentials, that he simply used one verse of song to get him onto the stage and one quick chorus to get him off. The burden of the act was this patter, which he rattled off as though he were having a cosy gossip with each and every member of the audience individually.

In pantomime, which took up the first quarter of every year, the characters he portrayed were all highly individual, but they were, of necessity, limited by the story of the pantomime and by the fact that he was playing with a host of other character comedians. His pantomime performances were painted with broad strokes: the characters were clearly defined, but not closely defined. In the music hall, where he spent three-quarters of every year, in a twenty minute turn he was able to give a concentrated, detailed, minutely-observed characterisation. He came on to sing a song, but the song itself was really irrelevant, it simply served to punctuate the apparently inconsequential chatter through which he managed to give so precise an impression of the person he was impersonating that you honestly felt you had known them—and loved them or loathed them—for years. In pantomime, where he was working with hundreds of other artistes (and animals too), where he was tied (albeit loosely) to a specific script, where he was competing with music and spectacle, and where he was having to appeal to children as well as to adults from every walk of life, literally from dustmen to dukes, his performance was much more of a crude burlesque, bereft of subtlety and cutting edge. But in the music hall, where his audience was more homogeneous, and where he was there alone on stage, without competitors and without distractions, he was able to dig much deeper and reveal much more.

Very few of the songs he sang and used as the basis for his characterisations were actually written by him. His own most successful effort was a parody of a number called 'Queen of my Heart', the original of which, when sung by Hayden Coffin at the Prince of Wales Theatre, had been the saving of a comic opera called *Dorothy*. Dan's version was entitled 'I'll give him beans tonight' and he sang it in the guise of a shrewish wife sitting up in the night waiting to welcome her truant husband home. But although most of his songs were composed and written by others, he could claim to have been part-author of all of them, because having bought a song he made it all his own, to the extent that the original author, as one of them admitted, 'was fain to confess that, although the ground plan was his, the building belonged to Dan Leno'.

Getting the right ground plan was important to Dan. He claimed to buy the rights in every song that was ever sent to him. This was not exactly true, but he certainly bought very many more than he actually decided to use and build upon. He told one interviewer, 'I have fully 150 songs at home for which I have paid from one to five guineas each, and which are utterly useless. Sometimes I sit up all night studying a song, and trying to see chances of effect in it, until I finally get out of temper and throw it in the fire. I study hard for all my songs, and my favourite way of doing that is to walk for a few miles in the rain, keeping time with my feet to the tune.'

When Dan made his first adult appearance at a London music hall, when he made his debut in pantomime at the Surrey and at the Lane, he appeared as a woman. Dan's women were neither the glamorous creations of a drag artist, nor the bluff and beefy types of the 'I'm-really-a-bloke-in-skirts' school of pantomime dame. They were, of their kind and class—none too young, none too pretty, none too fancy, none too bright, indomitable despite all the odds—real women. They were women that women recognised as women and women that men felt they knew all too well.

Herbert Darnley, who was responsible for many of Dan's later successes, wrote and composed a song called 'I'll Marry Him' in which Dan portrayed what might be called the essential Leno woman. Ostensibly the song dealt with a certain lady's determination to marry a somewhat reluctant suitor who worked in the building trade and went by the name of Jim Johnson. The opening verse, patter and chorus went like this:

For twenty-five years I've been doing my best
  To make with Jim Johnson a match;
I've done everything except ask him point-blank,
  But he won't come up to the scratch.
I really think Jim's very partial to me,
  Though never a word has he said;
But this morning I passed where he's building a house,
  And he threw half a brick at my head.

Spoken: Just to call my attention. You know we've been courting a long time—at least, I've done the courting; Jim's so slow. You see, I do very well in my business. I'm a dressmaker's labourer. I think Jim's awfully fond of me. I'm very fond of Jim, but I can't stand his sister; she's so mean. Oh! she is a mean woman. She's so mean that she'll buy half-a-dozen oysters and eat them in front of a looking-glass to make them look like a dozen. But she shan't turn me against Jim.

Chorus:

My mind's made up, I'm going to marry him;
  He'll have to come to church; if he won't I'll carry him.
Five-and-twenty years I've had my eye on Jim;
  If he won't marry me, I'll marry him.

At the end of the third verse, apropos of nothing and almost by the way, he introduced a character called Mrs. Kelly:

You see, we had a row once, and it was all through Mrs.

Kelly. You know Mrs. Kelly, of *course*—Mrs. Kelly—*Mrs. Kelly*! ! *You* know Mrs. Kelly? Of, you *must* know Mrs. Kelly! Good life a-mighty! Don't look so simple. She's a cousin of Mrs. Niplett's, and her husband keeps the little what-not shop at the—oh! you must know Mrs. Kelly. Everybody knows Mrs. Kelly!

Indeed, in next to no time everybody did know her—and knew her well. He spoke of her so knowingly and with such conviction that, in a moment, he managed to convince his audience that they knew her quite as intimately as he did. Mrs. Kelly became real, so real, in fact, that poor Jim Johnson was quite forgotten and the song quickly rechristened 'Mrs. Kelly'. Such was the strength of Dan's power of suggestion that Mrs. Kelly immediately assumed a life and identity of her own. Dan was delighted that people would come up to him in the street and ask after her—enquiring about a lady they had never seen and who had never existed except in Dan's imagination.

If husbands recognised their wives in Leno's women and women recognised their neighbours (assuming that, much as they warmed to the characters, none actually saw them as themselves), men could recognise their workmates and women their husbands in Leno's men. In the same way that many of his wives were put-upon and browbeaten, so many of his husbands were harried and hen-pecked. They were as gossipy as their wives, but Dan did not allow them to be quite as sentimental. Here is a snatch of patter from 'The Grass Widower':

And the wife's gone away for a week! . . . She turned round and said: 'You brute! You massive brute! I believe you wish I was dead!' (Isn't it funny how wives guess your thoughts!) I said: 'No, darling, but you must hurry up and get your train in the morning.'
So I put the clock on four hours—we had to get up before we went to bed. But when I got to the station, I couldn't contain myself. I felt so overjoyed, I could have cuddled the engine. And I got hold of the guard, and I said: 'What time does it go?' He

says: 'In five minutes.' I said: 'Make it off in two, and there's a pot of four-half for you!' He says: 'Shall I lock the lady in?' I said: 'Nail her in! Hammer her in!'

And here is the rather more pathetic Mr. Pipkins in a song with words by Harry King, who wrote a number of Dan's earlier successes, and music by George Le Brunn, who was responsible for much of the music in the pantomimes at the Lane. The bain of Mr. Pipkins's life is not only his wife, but also every comic's favourite butt, his mother-in-law.

How me met, 'twas quite romantic, in the Maze of Hampton Court;
Love, I thought, would drive me frantic, in three weeks the ring I bought.
A peck of rice, a bag of slippers, brought but one small week of bliss.
Ma-in-law she came to see us; then my hair came out like this—

Patter: That's her mother's doing. 'Pon my word, I don't know whether I'm married to the mother or daughter sometimes. Oh, they do beat me, and, of course you daren't hit a woman; well, I know I daren't. I can assure you I'm one mass of bruises; if my coat wasn't sewn on me I could show you some lovely bruises. I suppose it's because I enjoy bad health that I bruise so nice. I don't know what I wanted to get married for. Yet I might have done worse; I might have got run over or poisoned. My life's one long wretchedness; and it's

All through a woman with a coal-black eye,
All through a woman who was false and sly,
For when she said she lov'd me,
She told a wicked lie;
And her mother's at the bottom of it all!

From the patter that followed the third verse of the song, you get a sense of the way in which Dan liked to pile the ludicrous on top of the unlikely and then heap the fantastic on top of the ludicrous:

Now I'm always in hot water, nothing that I do is right.
If I row, my eldest daughter brings her young man home to fight.
I've been bruised from top to bottom, yet compelled to keep it dark;
They took care I always got 'em where you couldn't see the mark.

Patter: It was very strange that I should first meet my wife in the Maze. I'd never been in the Maze before (well I've never been out of one since). I think every married man's a bit mazy, more or less. Well, to make a long story thick, I was walking up and down, and after walking for about two hours I found I hadn't moved; somehow or other I'd mislaid myself. I tried to find a side door at the back, but no. Then it struck me all of a lump that I was lost. Well it's dangerous to lose a person like me. So I began to cry, when some one over the other side of the hedge said, 'Don't cry, little boy, here's some nuts.' Oh, I was so pleased that I was found; and when I found it was a lady that was speaking, I shall never forget how I felt. I went all of a cold perspiration and I said, 'I ain't a little boy.' She said, 'I beg your pardon.' I said, 'You're welcome.' So one word got to another; then she told me my name, and I told her hers. I asked her to go for a stroll when we got outside; she said she'd be delighted a lot, but how was she to know me? I said, 'When we get out I'll cough twice.' So when I got out I coughed a lovely cough, and the man at the gate said, 'You've got hydrophobia.' I said, 'I beg to differ,' and then up came the girl. Oh, I was so bashful. I asked her to have some wine, so she ordered a pot of shandy gaff. I said, 'No, let's have two.' So I ordered two pots of gandy-shaff. I gave the waiter half a sovereign—no, let me see—fourpence; I get mixed a little. Then I ordered tea. I said, 'What will you have for tea?' She said, 'Anything you like.' So I ordered two plates of anything you like, and cruffins and mumpets. Oh, and we did have a game! I burnt her hand with a teaspoon and threw the watercress at the waiter, and she filled my cup with salt and I was sick. Oh, we did enjoy ourselves! Then we went home. But after leaving her I couldn't rest, nor eat my supper. I had to call my landlady up to sit with me a couple of hours. She said, 'Lor! Mr. Pipkins, what's the matter with you?' and I told her I'd met my divinity. She said, 'Lor! have a mustard plaster on at once.' I said, 'No, it's my sweetheart.' And I do believe if her mother hadn't have interfered we should have been happy. But! Lor, married life makes a man of you. Before I was married I didn't dare say a word; now look at the difference, I daren't open my mouth at all now; and it's

All through a woman, etc.

The technique of piling absurdity upon absurdity at an ever-increasing speed was one he frequently used. The audience would listen, spell-bound, holding its breath, unwilling to laugh until the end for fear of breaking the momentum. You can see the temperature rising and the pace quickening in this extract from 'My Wife's Relations':

. . . And—er—during that time, our stepfather had married a third mother, and he'd pre-deceased also our second mother. So my brother met our third mother, fell in love with her and married her.

Well now, that's where the trouble commenced. Because, you see, that made me my brother's son, and my sister-in-law was really my mother. Well now then, follow me closely, will you? There was an aunt by marriage—she had an adopted daughter. Left to her for rent, or something. And—er—the—this daughter fell in love with the man that built the house where our second mother lives. You see where we're getting to? Well now then, keep close to me, will you? This is rather intricate. You see the uncle—oh! Oh, no, no, I'm wrong! I—no—yes—that's right! Oh, and—er—and there was a postman in it as well.

Decades before I.T.M.A., the Goons and Monty Python, Dan Leno was revelling in the absurd. He used verbal, visual and imaginative lunacy in a way that surprised his contemporaries and yet delighted them. When he turned up at a rehearsal of *Mother Goose* with a song called 'The Wasp and the Hard-Boiled

Egg', none of the company could quite believe it. The concept was absurd; it was something that the literal Victorian mind could not visualise—although it could appreciate it when offered it by a mind as fabulous as, say, that of Lewis Carroll or Edward Lear or, in his genre, Dan Leno. The company chuckled at the thought of 'The Wasp and the Hard-Boiled Egg' because it made no sense to them, but Leno had a way of making nonsense make sense to insensibly 'sensible' people, and he sang the song throughout the run of the pantomime. According to Hickory Wood, who wrote the *Mother Goose*, it was a great success. 'Who that heard him can ever forget the pathos—almost amounting to tears—in his voice, when, after the passionate appeal of the wasp to the hard-boiled egg, he sang:

> But not one word said the hard-boiled egg,
> The hard-boiled egg,
> The hard-boiled egg,
> And what a silly insect the wasp to beg!
> For you can't get any sense out of a hard-boiled egg?

It could never occur to anybody but a Dan Leno to create such an incompatible alliance as a wasp and a hard-boiled egg, and make a mock ballad out of the result.'

He made a great feature of eggs (though not of wasps) in one of his most successful songs 'Our Stores', which he wrote in collaboration with Harry Wright, and in which he portrayed a grocer's assistant obsessed with the ethics of egg-selling:

> Where is there an article that will compel you to tell more lies than an egg? Do you know, I don't think we properly grasp eggs. There is something awfully artful about an egg—there is a mystery in it. Of course, there are three kinds of eggs—there is the new-laid egg (which is nearly extinct)—then there is the fresh egg, which is almost the same as the new-laid, but with an additional something about it that makes all the difference. Then comes The Egg; that is the egg I am talking about. That is the egg that causes all the trouble. It's only a little round white thing, but you can't tell what it's thinking about. You daren't kick it, and you daren't drop it. It has got

no face. You can't get it to laugh. You simply look at it and say, 'Egg!'

'This morning a lady came in and said, "How do you sell eggs?" I said, "As quickly as possible." She walked out again.

'On New Year's Day I made a lot of good resolutions. I made up my mind that, whatever happened, I would always speak the truth—whatever happened, I would never tell another lie as long as I lived—and I was feeling so happy and comfortable and angelic about it as I was taking down the shutters in the morning, when—What do you think? What do you think? The very first customer who came into the shop asked me straight out. "Are those eggs fresh?"'

And not another word did he utter. He just spread out his hands in a hopeless, helpless gesture that told the rest of the story.

He could imbue inanimate objects with a life of their own—of a cake he'd say, 'It looks as if it's got an extremely obstinate nature, but I think you'll enjoy that speck of jam in the middle'—and people a whole stage with invisible characters that you felt you could see quite as clearly as he obviously saw them himself. In 'The Shopwalker', for example, he scored one of his greatest triumphs, and had his audience in fits, not because the piece was intrinsically funny—it contained no 'jokes' at all—but because he managed to make his audience believe not just in the shopwalker himself, but in the customers he was addressing as well:

Ladies' gloves, sir?—thank you! Take a chair?—thank you. Something about half-a-sovereign? No? One-and-six? I'm afraid we haven't any at that price. Oh, yes! there's some in the window, but they're only glued to the glass. Try these, I'm sure they will give you terrible satisfaction. Two pairs?—sure you won't have the half-dozen? No?—thank you! Black tie?—thank you! For yourself—thank you! Would you like a nice white with a blue stripe? Black?—thank you! Perhaps you would like one of our new shades—'pink puce'—very becoming! No? Black?—thank you! Are you quite sure no other colour would do—quite sure? Well, I'm very sorry we are out of black; we shall have some in, in about a fortnight.

Nothing else? Good morning! Nice shower after the rain! Walk this way, madam! Take a chair—thank you! Beautiful weather, don't it? What can I get for you? Some flimsey woolsey?—thank you! Two yards?—thank you! Sure two yards will be sufficient?—thank you! Now the next thing? Flannel petticoats?—thank you! Oh, I can recommend these, my wife wears them winter and summer. Two?—thank you! Now the next?—oh, you may speak with confidence, I have a daughter as old as yourself—I understand! White, I suppose?

But this character never became too true to be funny and his *non sequiturs* never became so fantastic that they left the audience behind. He wanted, indeed, longed for the laughs and willingly accepted them even when they came in a conventionally straightforward way. Here are a couple of moments from 'The Recruiting Sergeant' in which the jokes are nothing if not obvious:

'What a life! Oh, my word! Splendid life! Nothing to do but stand still and walk about all day! Dear, oh dear! A wonderful life! I was standing at the corner of the street the other day, and I saw a fine, handsome, dashing fellow—a man much after my own stamp. I thought what a fine soldier he would make. I walked over to him and said, "You want to be a soldier?" He said, "I don't. I'm waiting for a bus!" Oh dear! Oh dear! My word! What a life!

'The other day I was standing at another corner of the street —I always stand at corners, because then I catch them both ways. A fine young fellow came up and said, "Governor, will I do for a soldier?" I said, "I think so!" I walked round him, and I noticed he walked round at the same time. When I got him before the doctor, the doctor said, "Smirks! you do find them," and we discovered he'd only one arm. Well I'd never noticed it because, you see, he kept the arm behind him that he hadn't got.'

And some of the jokes in 'The Waiter'—a turn which involved him darting from imaginary table to imaginary table in so life-like a way that you could almost hear the plates clatter and the cutlery rattle—are still being used today. If you have not heard at least three of the gags in this routine on radio or television, in 'panto' or a seaside summer show, you cannot have been listening very carefully:

'Pon my word, some people think a waiter's on wheels. I've worn myself down to a point. I've got no feet. I've worn 'em off. I've had to have the bottom of my legs turned up to make feet. These trousers were knicker-bockers when I came here first. And what you have to put up with! Yesterday a gentleman came in and wanted a steak. I brought it. Then he said he couldn't get his teeth in it. No wonder! he'd only got false ones, and those he'd put in his coat-tail pocket. I told him he'd have to sit on the steak to eat it, if he kept his teeth in his pocket. Then another gentleman orders a spring chicken and a bottle of '64 port, and when I bring them he won't pay for them, because he says they are spring port and '64 chicken. My word, instead of giving a man seven years for life, they should make a waiter of him. Yes, sir, I'm coming, sir! How long will your steak be? Oh, about four inches, sir! No, we don't keep toothpicks, we lose so many of them; people used to use them and take 'em away, sir. I don't know what you're going to do—use your umbrella or fork. Coming, sir! What's the matter with the tripe? Green! Oh, yes, that's the only colour we keep now; we don't keep the common unbleached tripe—find it very nice, sir—we keep it in the same cellar as the gorgonzola. Coming, sir! What! the chop smells? Can't, sir, I've brought that chop up to four people today, sir! Never noticed it before! it must be your mouth out of taste, sir! Oh, no! I could not change it! You see, you've stuck your fork in it—you've let the steam out! Sir! yes, I know it smells, I can hear it myself, but I can't change it. Didn't know you wanted to smell it; thought you wanted to eat it! You must put plenty of pepper on it and hold your nose and eat it quick; it will soon go! Yes, sir! coming, sir! Your bill! let me see, you've had one call—one beef, one cheese —What, sir, no cheese? I brought cheese, I know! I see it! it's going downstairs again! You ought to have kept your foot on it. Never mind, sir! charge you a little extra for letting it go; comes to sixteen and six, sir. Wrong, is it! let me see. Oh, of course! I'm wrong; you had no butter—my mistake; comes to three and fourpence. Thank you, sir. He's a good sort—given me a tanner! it's a shirt button—more swindling! When he comes in again I'll empty a basin of soup over him!

With Leno, the timing was impeccable. When he told you about his parents who laid in a stock of gunpowder to make fireworks for Guy Fawkes' Night and someone had dropped a lighted match on it making it explode and sending his parents shooting out through the roof—he'd pause just long enough to force the audience to hold its breath and then deliver the pay-off: 'the first time they'd been out together for years.'

In another of his biggest hits, a Herbert Darnley number called 'The Beefeater', he used telling pauses to build the dramatic tension and heighten the absurdity as he gradually made the audience aware that although he claimed to be showing visitors round the Tower of London, he was really intent on luring them elsewhere:

There's not a place on the face of the earth like the Tower of London. If you've never been there, go again. It's a glorious place, and supplies a long felt want. Everything old. And the first ancient item you meet is the man that takes your money at the door. Then you pass through the Refreshment Room, which is the oldest Refreshment Room in the Tower, and the only one. And there's some very ancient items in the Refreshment Room, such as the buns, and the ginger beer, and the barmaids and whatnot.

Good-day, ladies! Do you want to see the Tower? Splendid day to see the Tower—nice and gloomy! Now—er—in the first place, this is the Refreshment Room. Er—of course, if you want anything in the Refreshment Room, now is the time. You don't care for anything? No? Thank you! Only as we go along, there's no oranges or ginger beer to be had, and of course, if you feel faint, you have to come back to the Refreshment Room. You . . . No . . . you don't care? No . . . Don't want anything? No . . . I do! Still—we'll proceed. Standing with our backs to the Refreshment Room, we get a lovely view of the Tower. Follow me, ladies. Standing with your backs to the Tower, you get a lovely view of . . . er . . . the Refreshment Room. Now you see that man there? That's the sentry. He stands there night and day with his gun fixed, bayonet fixed and his eyes always on one spot . . . and this is—er—the Refreshment Room.

Obviously much of his skill had been acquired during the twenty years he had spent on the road before coming to the London halls, but there was more to his timing than the conventional know-how acquired through playing the roughest, toughest audiences in public house concert rooms and provincial variety theatres. He used pauses differently from the average stand-up comedian. He was much more daring. In his hilarious satire on the Scots and the 'gathering of the clans' he would start the chorus very jauntily:

There were McGregor's men,
And McPherson's men,
And McTulloch's men,
And Mc——

At this juncture his memory failed him. Confronted by this sudden mental aberration he allowed his face a momentary twinge of distress, pulled himself together and started all over again:

There were McGregor's men,
And McPherson's men,
And McTulloch's men,
And Mc——

It simply wouldn't come. He did his best to jolt his memory into life, but to no avail. He made one more valiant attempt, got stuck at precisely the same point and gave up.

'Never mind! On with the dance!'

And as the band struck up he threw himself into the highest and most outlandish Highland fling imaginable, in the very midst of which his expression changed dramatically as a thought struck him like a thunderbolt. He stopped. He clapped his hands. The band stopped. He walked confidently down to the footlights, announced 'McFarlane's men!' and, without further ado, walked off. The brilliance of the effect lay not just in the timing of the line, but in the audacity of walking straight off the stage immediately after it: no more song, no more dance, nothing but a clean exit.

He played on the London halls for almost twenty years and in that time created a wide range of comic characters—the Railway Guard, the Doctor, the Detective, the Fireman, the Huntsman, the Professor of Anatomy, the Cobbler, the County Councillor, the Cavalier, the Jap, the Ice-Cream Man, the Seaside Holiday-maker, One of the Unemployed, as well as every variety of abused parent, garrulous wife and henpecked husband—all of whom shared a basic humanity, simplicity, homeliness and unmistakable proximity to the man in the street. He was a satirist who was clearly on the side of those he satirised. Such was the burning intensity of what he had to say and his breathless anxiety in saying it, that the audience longed to hear his confidences, sympathise with his pent-up indignation and share his sense of surprise at the awfulness and absurdity of the world.

If his magic would not work for us now it could be because he immortalised the failures, not the successes of his generation, and audiences in our day do not see themselves as failures at all. Dan Leno personified the underdog who refused to go under and his audiences in the main were folk who accepted that they too were underdogs and he encouraged them to realise that they need not go under either. A working-class Victorian and his wife in a crowded, beery, noisy, smoke-filled music hall in the Shaftesbury Avenue or the Mile End Road of the 1890s could identify with the world Dan Leno created for them on stage. A working-class couple today, watching a colour television in the comparative luxury of the 1970s, would not want to identify with Dan Leno's world. They have moved on to 'better' things.

And what is more, what was original when Dan Leno did it first seems hackneyed now. Just as yesterday's new-minted turn of phrase becomes today's cliché, so too not only the material he used but the way in which he used it have become a part of the common currency of all comics since his day. Long before audiences laughed at the vulnerable pomposity of Tony Hancock, long before the inspired lunacy of the likes of Spike Milligan became predictable, long before Larry Grayson introduced us to his friends Everard and Slack Alice and Apricot Lil, long before Frankie Howerd took us into his confidence with his stammering ooos and aaahs, Leno had originated the techniques modern audiences feel, understandably, comedians like these have made their own. (And if proof is needed, just picture for a moment either Grayson or Howerd telling us, each in his own way, 'You know Mrs. Kelly, of *course*—Mrs. Kelly—*Mrs. Kelly!! You* know Mrs. Kelly? Good life a-mighty! Don't look so simple. She's a cousin of Mrs. Niplett's and her husband keeps the little what-not shop at the—oh! you must know Mrs. Kelly'. It works.)

But there was more to the Leno magic than originality, timing and technique. There was another ingredient, the indefinable one that makes you realise the moment you see two different performers of apparently equal skill that one of them 'has it' and the other one hasn't. 'It needs no courage or jugglery of speech to say that Dan Leno was a genius,' wrote Wilfred Whitten as 'John o' London' in his obituary in *T.P.'s Weekly*. 'Let anyone call up the scene and atmosphere of one of his performances, and then shut his eyes and remember and compare, and he will see that Dan Leno brought something to the stage that was not in his song or in his talk, or anything of his nameable qualities; not even in his humour. None of these really distinguished him from the other. Behind all lay a unique quality to which one cannot put a word.'

In the last quarter of the twentieth century, when hyperbole is the order of the day and we like to have a word for everything, we would probably call it 'star quality'. Plenty of performers get star billing who do not have star quality: the one feature shared by the handful of entertainers with true star quality is that you cannot take your eyes off them. They compel you to look at them. Dan Leno was like that. When he was on stage, there was not a moment when he did not have the audience tight in his power. They could not get away from him. They did not quite know why and he did not quite know why, but he held them in his thrall.

CHAPTER FIVE

The Funniest Man on Earth

Towards the end of March 1897 huge posters were pasted up on hoardings all over New York announcing the imminent arrival of

DAN LENO
THE FUNNIEST MAN ON EARTH

Dan was thirty-six, at the height of his powers and the height of his fame, and ready to take America by storm. He did not quite make it.

His New York debut on 12 April at Hammerstein's Olympia Music Hall on Broadway was certainly a success, but only a qualified one. While there was no doubt that to an Englishman Dan Leno really *was* the funniest man on earth, native New Yorkers could be forgiven for feeling that they might have a few home-grown talents just as worthy of the title. The advance publicity brought in the crowds, but it also caused resentment, and no doubt contributed to the condescending tone of press notices like this one:

> It was absurd to presume that a London concert-hall singer could throw a New York audience into paroxysms of laughter. The jokes and the humour of the English vaudeville stage are, as a rule, so terribly out of date, that the importation of them to this country is apt to be a failure.
>
> Leno was fortunate that he ever made a good impression. It is easy to see, however, how, on his native soil, he became the idol of the people who attend the London concert halls. He is just the kind of an Englishman you would think would naturally appeal to Englishmen. He has just the manner and the

ways which every Englishman finds, for some reason or other, excruciatingly funny. In New York he is worth seeing only as a type—not a humorist. People unfamiliar with the English comique should find him interesting as a study.

But another New York paper was able to give a more generous account of the opening night:

When the New York public gets to know Dan Leno well, and Dan Leno gets to know the New York public well, there is no doubt about it, he'll be nearly as big a favourite here as he is on his native heath, meaning the London music-hall stage.

Every Englishman in the city, and many English women too, were at the Olympia last night to give Dan a welcome—and they gave it to him with a will.

A few minutes before he went on the stage, as he stood first on one foot and then on the other, and the beads of perspiration stood out all over his face, Mr. Leno remarked with a spasmodic smile that he was as cool as a cucumber, and felt as if he had been born and brought up right in New York.

Then he rubbed a little grease-paint on his cheeks, made a few dashes of black at the corners of his mouth and round his eyes, pulled on a pair of trousers, a vest, and a coat, each of them a mile too big, and he was ready for his first song, 'The Lucky Horseshoe.'

Meantime the audience was making all the noise it could—the way a New York audience always does when a new actor with a big European reputation makes his debut. Suddenly Leno makes a dash into the centre of the stage, and the applause redoubles. Then it is all quiet, and the song begins. At the end, there is some applause, but an American remarks—

'Well, I've heard better!'

The next song, 'Wait till I'm his Father', goes better; but still it is the Englishmen who lead the cheering. 'The North Pole' is voted decidedly slow by the Americans anyway, and then comes 'Going out of Town', which describes the joys of a man whose wife has been ordered away somewhere for her health. That is a situation every man present apparently understands perfectly, and before the song is half over the house is roaring its approval, and Dan Leno has made his hit.

'The Shop-Walker' goes even better. Such droll mimicry, such grotesque pantomime, New Yorkers had not seen before, and—well—you've all heard of deafening applause: that's what followed the performance.

One lady in a box almost had hysterics, and gave vent to her feelings by shouting—

'Give 'em "The Red Poppies", Dan!'

And Dan forthwith proceeded to oblige.

That closed Mr. Leno's turn, and four big floral pieces were passed over the footlights, while the audience shouted for a speech. Mr. Leno was visibly affected, and, when he could make himself heard, he explained that he had been a little bit nervous at first, but that was all over now, and he hoped to show his appreciation of the public's kindness on future occasions. Flowers were usually sent to the beautiful, and he presumed——with an unusually grotesque twist of his features—that was why he had been so favoured.

To top off the whole, he gave an amusing little recitation about 'The Robin Redbreast', and danced a hornpipe. Then he retired, while the audience yelled itself hoarse, and clapped its hands sore.

Although Dan used to say regularly that he considered his visit to America 'the crown of my career', he was very relieved when his month-long engagement in New York came to an end. It had been a 'wonderful experience', but not one he chose to repeat. He was frequently asked to work abroad, notably, of course, in the United States and Australia, but he declined all the offers, and they were lucrative ones, without apparent regret. Apart from his four weeks on Broadway, Dan Leno never appeared—or even went—abroad.

In Britain now wherever Dan played he was top of the bill—and they were bills that included all the great names from the hey-day of British music hall. For an old-fashioned silver shilling, you could go to the Tivoli or the Oxford, the Pavilion or the Empire or the Alhambra, and see the likes of Marie Lloyd, Albert Chevalier, Lottie Collins, Dutch Daly, George Robey, Little Tich, Harry Lauder, Vesta Tilley, Bransby Williams and a dozen more on the same stage on the same night. In fact, if you felt so inclined, you could follow your favourite artiste from hall to hall and see them three or four times in the same evening.

In addition to topping the bill at music halls and variety theatres throughout the land, Dan made the occasional appearance in high society. At a price you could hire him as an after-dinner entertainer for the party at your country seat or West End mansion, or you could lure him to come for nothing in aid of a good cause, but Dan was never quite at home playing to audiences entirely composed of nobs. He did not really understand them and he knew that they did not always understand him. He used to tell the tale of how, after one of these rare private appearances for the benefit of the exclusive and the wealthy, he was cornered in the retiring room by the well-intentioned son of the house:

> I say, Mr. Leno, I must tell you how much I enjoyed your comic songs. I think they are awfully good, and I can assure you I laughed immensely. They were ripping—every one of them; but there was one that I liked, if possible, better than any of the others. I forget the name of it, and I'm not quite sure what it was about; but I know you mentioned a frying-pan in it, and that appealed to me very much; I quite understood that one, because I've seen a frying-pan, don't you know.

As well as making countless appearances as a solo act and performing in eighteen London pantomimes, Dan Leno appeared in four musical comedies. The first was an improbable piece of nonsense set in Ancient Greece called *Atalanta*. It was written by George P. Hawtrey, starred William F. Hawtrey as Schoeneus, King of Scyros, and was presented at the Strand Theatre by C. H. Hawtrey. When the burlesque opened on 17 November 1888 Dan Leno was not in the cast. He, along with Alma Stanley and a couple of others, were recruited to strengthen the company later in the month following the opening and poor press reception.

Dan took over the part of Leontes from Miss Florence Lancaster and though the part was not a big one his performance was generally well received, and many regarded his Olympic stage race with Alma Stanley 'the fleet-footed' as the highlight of the evening. 'He brings a good deal of fun and quaintness to the not very important part of Leontes . . . Moreover, his singing and dancing are good helps to the performance,' was the verdict of the critic from the *Illustrated Sporting and Dramatic News*. (In the same notice, the reviewer offers a sharp rebuke to the ladies of the chorus, 'It would be better if some of the ladies did not look about so much and did a little less talking', thus giving a useful indication of the production's general standard.) That Dan did strengthen the company of *Atalanta* is made quite apparent from the verse that was published parodying one of the songs of Tom Squire, who was also in the show:

> The booking went up, up, up,
> They came from all over the town;
> But when Stanley or Leno
> Were not to be seen, oh!
> The booking went down, down, down.

The Hawtreys were understandably anxious to keep Dan in the cast, but as he was already under contract to Augustus Harris and due to make his Drury Lane debut at Christmas, and Harris had no intention of releasing him and he had no desire to be released, he had to leave *Atalanta* after playing in it for less than a month and allow it to die its natural death without him.

It was ten years before Dan appeared in another such show, but this time the vehicle was not one that he was dragged on to in order to rescue it: it was 'his' show, custom-built as a showcase for his peculiar talents. The piece was called *Orlando Dando* and it was the brainchild of the impressario Milton Bode, who sensed a potential gold-mine in touring the provinces with an extravagant musical comedy built around the greatest music hall star of the day. He approached Dan with the idea in 1896 only to be told by Dan's agent that his client was both very busy and very expensive. Indeed, he was booked up solidly for the next two years and four months, and even when he did become available he had only six weeks to spare for which he would expect at least £125. When Bode declared that he would be more than happy to book him for those six weeks and quite willing to pay the salary asked, and even prepared to offer an immediate advance of £500, Dan in person stepped in to say he would be delighted to sign the contract right away.

The contract was duly signed, the twenty-eight months duly elapsed and when 1898 duly arrived, Dan undertook the tour. It was a great triumph. Such a triumph, in fact, that Milton Bode readily re-engaged Dan for a further tour the following year to play Aubrey Honeybun, an incompetent detective, in a 'new musical farce' called *In Gay Piccadilly!* In 1902 Dan went on his last tour for Milton Bode in a third piece entitled *Mr. Wix of Wickham*. As drama, none of the shows bore close critical inspection: but as three-hour extravaganzas through which Dan Leno, thinly disguised as Messrs. Dando or Honeybun or Wix, could caper, singing his songs, dancing his dances and chatting of this and that in his own hilarious way, they were ideal.

All this work brought him considerable fame and fortune. He revelled in both. He never tired of meeting his public in person, of being greeted in the street, of signing autographs and posing for photographers. Such was his fame and the potency of his name that both a saloon bar and a comic newspaper were named after him, and he was delighted to open the former in person—at the Scarbro' Hotel in Leeds—and appear to be the actual editor of the latter.

Dan Leno's Comic Journal was one of the very first papers to be launched on the strength of the name of an actual individual. Published by C. Arthur Pearson, Issue Number 1 appeared on 26 February 1898 and sold an impressive 350,000 copies. It was an eight-page tabloid with the slogan 'One Touch of Leno Makes the Whole World Grin'. 'Won't wash clothes, but will mangle melancholy' was another page one promise and for a mere halfpenny you got a week's worth of chuckles. The cover showed a drawing of Dan and his editorial staff at work and play and the inside pages featured 'Daniel's Diary', 'Moans from the Martyr' by 'Daniel Junior', two gripping yarns, a couple of dozen cartoons and 'Leno's Latest—Fresh Jokes and Wheezes Made on the Premises'. The jokes were anything but fresh, of course, but, for the early issues at least, Dan actually contributed a few himself and several were rather funny:

LULU: You should get him to sign the pledge before you marry him.

BABA: Why, he doesn't drink.

LULU: No, but he may be tempted to do so later.

HORRIFIED OLD LADY: Oh, kind sir, think of your mother! Think of your mother!

BURGLAR [*sternly*]: No use, lady—I was brought up in an incubator.

EMPLOYER [*angrily*]: What are you throwing those handbills on the pavement for?

BILL DISTRIBUTOR: Well, guv'nor, that's wot the people does as I gives 'em to. So it's only saving time.

Nothing personal to Dan could appear in the paper without his vetting it first and according to Peter Keary, the man from Pearson's whose idea the comic had been and who was responsible for the negotiations with Leno, 'he killed a good deal of stuff every week'. At the beginning Dan took a very real interest in the paper and a pride in its popularity, contributed ideas and material and did his best to help boost the circulation, but once the novelty had worn off, he gradually lost interest in the project and, after a run of almost two years, Pearson's allowed it to die.

The demise of *Dan Leno's Comic Journal* didn't quite mark the end of Dan's career as an 'editor'. In 1902 the proprietors of the London evening newspaper the *Sun* had the bright idea of inviting Dan to edit the paper on April Fools' Day, with Herbert Campbell engaged as Deputy Editor. On 1 April the *Sun* still bore its regular legend 'If you see it in the *Sun* it is so', but, for once, if you saw it in the *Sun* it obviously was not so. Dan contributed an editorial rich in homespun philosophy ('When your face wants to slide into a smile, let it; when it doesn't want to, make it. A merry minded man is a perpetual slab of sunshine and brightens up the work-a-day world a sight more than a circus procession or a check-suit'), jokes, parodies and phoney news items. The paper's sales were doubtless increased that day, but the readers must have been confused as well as entertained, for alongside many of the joke news items were real ones and, in some instances, telling the two apart cannot have been easy.

In 1899 Greening & Co. published a 'volume of frivolities, autobiographical, historical, philosophical, anecdotal and nonsensical' under the title *Dan Leno: Hys Booke* and ostensibly 'written by himself'. In fact it was the work of a young writer called T. C. Elder. Dan cooperated in the venture and supplied Mr. Elder with a number of facts and numerous anecdotes for the book, but he did not write a word of it himself and cannot have read the proofs very carefully, if at all, as errors—starting with his date of birth being given with the wrong day, the wrong month and the wrong year!—abound on almost every page.

Nevertheless when the book appeared Dan, who naturally received a royalty on every copy sold, did his best to promote it and never revealed that it had been ghosted for him. Indeed it was not until many years after his death that the secret of the book's authorship was revealed—and there are many people who still assume, most understandably, that it is all Dan's work. (For example, in 1977 the Victoria and Albert Museum had a copy on display and stated that it was by Dan himself, giving the incorrect date of birth mentioned in the book, and an American scholar produced a thesis on Lenoesque humour using Mr. Elder's witty prose as evidence.) All the same the book, more anecdotal and nonsensical than autobiographical and historical, is easy, entertaining reading and quickly became a best-seller.

But Dan was not only immortalised in print. He was also preserved in china and earthenware (with Dan Leno jugs, Dan Leno mugs, even Dan Leno inkwells!) and on celluloid. Birt Acres, the pioneer film-maker who later turned his talents to perfecting and producing film projectors, made three short pictures of Dan (on the stage, at home and playing in a charity cricket match), none of which has survived. As well as appearing in Acres's films, Dan also took part in a long-distance Command

Performance on 24 May 1899 in which he was the third item on the programme and sang a song in St. James's Hall in London that was 'transmitted by wire to Windsor by means of the electrophone' where it was heard by Queen Victoria and her guests as part of the celebrations marking the Queen's eightieth birthday.

The only manifestations of Leno at work that still exist today are some of the many records he made right at the start of the century. They give no flavour at all of what he must have been like, partly because the quality of the recordings is so poor and the reproduction so primitive, but largely because the recordings were made at the City Road offices of the Gramophone and Typewriter Company to an audience of six lads from the firm's packing room. Performing cold, first thing in the morning, with no notion of how to handle a recording session, Dan's records are dismal to listen to. He was no great singer, his patter depended largely for its effect on the response of the audience, and he was essentially a visual entertainer—on stage he never stopped moving, when his arms came to a halt, his legs took over: he could leap back six feet in one stride and carry on singing—perfect in the atmosphere of the music hall. On a bleak Tuesday morning, standing stock still in front of a contraption he understood not a jot, without an audience, without a proper band, without his costume and his props, he was nothing. 'How the hell can I be funny into a funnel?' he asked when first confronted with the recording horn.

From Dan's point of view, the only drawback to his fame was that it led others to imitate him. He did not mind the amateurs who bought a Dan Leno song sheet and took it home to perform in the parlour for the benefit of their friends, but he bitterly resented those professionals who copied his act. The resentment was quite uncalled for, because every Dan Leno impersonation was an advertisement for Dan Leno and intended as a tribute and a compliment, and they were all destined to failure anyway because Dan was, as he himself knew, utterly inimitable. Sitting in the audience at a seaside concert party one afternoon, he was alarmed suddenly to hear the artiste on stage announce, 'I will now give my celebrated imitation of a gentleman who is at this moment among the audience—Mr. Dan Leno!' After the show,

Dan went backstage and gave the hapless impostor half-a-sovereign: 'This isn't for your talent; it's for your confounded cheek!'

If Dan was unreasonably harsh towards those who attempted open imitations of him, he justly despised those who stole his ideas and his material without acknowledgement: 'blasted thieves', he called them. Dan had a characteristic entrance onto the stage on the halls: he would run on quickly, rush down to the footlights, give a roll like a drum with his feet, lift up one leg, hold it in the air for a moment, then slap it down with a crack like a rifle-shot. On one memorable Saturday afternoon at the Tivoli, the young George Robey came on and copied Dan's entrance. A few turns later, Dan himself came on stage, ran down to the front as usual, gave the roll and the crack. Then he stopped dead and gave the roll and the crack once more. 'You see that?' he said to the audience. 'You saw something *like* that a little while ago—but it's *mine*!' George Robey never used Dan's entrance again, but he kept Dan's arched eyebrows to the end of his life.

Despite being the preeminent music hall star of his day, despite the proof of his success all around him, Dan never felt secure. 'Nobody cares for me—nobody!' was his cry. He used a press cutting service which supplied him with a set number of clippings for a guinea and read through every one assiduously, almost as though he were looking for an unkind comment so that he could be hurt by it. When he found one, he'd read it to Herbert Campbell who said, with some cause, 'Serve you right for buying a guinea's worth of trouble.'

He was sensitive to criticism and yet received hardly any. Indeed he was the subject of adulation that as often as not did not stop this side of idolatry. There cannot be many entertainers in the history of the world who have been able to read a notice like this, written not as an eulogistic obituary, but as a tribute to a working artiste:

> During the best part of the last half-century I have seen all the best, the drollest, the most pathetic and tragic comedians, whose humour, variety, tenderness, and intensity have delighted

the playgoers of the world. Among these representatives of art, and sometimes genius, Dan Leno holds his own bravely indeed. Nay, I am not sure that in certain gifts of expression, variety, and, if I may so express it, tornado or instant comic farce, Dan Leno has ever had a rival . . . He catches every expression, every trick, every attitude, every inflexion of voice, and all is done without offence or a suspicion of vulgarity. In his grim earnestness consists his humour.

Whenever he is on the stage, be it theatre or music-hall, he literally holds his audience tight in his power. They cannot get away from him.

He is monarch of all he surveys. Long, then, may the reign of King Dan Leno last; long may he be spared to us to delight the children at pantomime time, and to make those who, though going downhill, are not ashamed to laugh as young, at least in heart, as the little ones by their side.

The author of the piece was Clement Scott, dramatic critic of the *Daily Telegraph* from 1872 until shortly before his death in 1904, and not a man always easy to please. And Scott's panegyric was not an isolated effusion: the Leno family scrapbooks are filled with journalistic tributes just as lavish.

Along with his fame went considerable financial success. When he arrived in London in 1885 he was paid £5 a week for his first music hall engagement. Shortly before his death he had signed a contract with Moss Empires to undertake a tour of Birmingham, Liverpool and Leeds at a salary of £230 a week. With the proceeds from his personal appearances and the pantomimes, from the sale of the book and the records, from the fees paid to him for the right to use his name for promotional and advertising purposes, he was probably earning £20,000 a year at his peak, a substantial amount by today's standards, a fortune at the turn of the century. He earned more in a year than most of his contemporaries did in a lifetime, yet when he died he left only £10,994. The reason was simple: he spent a lot, he lost a lot and he gave a lot away.

He was recklessly generous. He gave away sums, large and

small, to almost anyone who cared to ask. When he walked through the street he tossed coins to the street urchins and handed money to nearly every beggar that crossed his path. Stanley Lupino was a boy without a penny in the world who got a gold half-sovereign from Dan when he saw him standing in the rain by the stage door of the London Pavilion. It was an act of kindness Lupino never forgot. Once, when Dan was appearing in Leeds, he received a pitiful letter from an old 'pro', claiming to be in a pathetic state of penury, without food, unable to pay the rent, having pawned all his possessions. Dan decided to check this particular story and went round to the man's house. He found it was all true, paid the rent, refurnished the whole house and stocked it with food. Many of the people who came up to him or wrote to him asking for help were frauds, but he gave the help nonetheless. 'There may be one deserving case among a dozen, so it's worth it,' he used to say.

Knowing his own reputation for ludicrous liberality, he would tell an amusing story against himself. Addressing a waiter in his club once, he said: 'Maurice, how long have you been working for this club?' 'Ever since it was started.' 'And what was the biggest tip you ever received?' 'Two sovereigns.' 'Well, my boy,' said Leno, 'I'll make that fellow look foolish. Here's a fiver! By-the-by, what was the name of the fellow who gave you two pounds?'

'Well, Mr. Leno,' said Maurice, after he had pocketed the note, 'it was yourself, sir.'

Doubtless remembering the deprivations of his own youth, he used his wealth and his position to help others as much as he could. He gave his time, his money and his services to countless charities—and particularly enjoyed playing the fool at comic charity cricket matches—and did what he could to improve the lot of his colleagues in the business. He was an active President of the Music Hall Benevolent Fund and, in February 1897, with Eugene Stratton, 'the Dandy Coloured Coon', and C. Douglas Stuart, the founder and editor of the *Encore*, formed the Music Hall Railway Rates Association which managed to secure railway fares for music hall artistes at seventy-five per cent of the normal rate, a privilege already enjoyed by legitimate actors. With Joe Elvin, Wal Pink, Jack Lotto, Harry Freeman and others he also was one of the founders of the 'Ancient Order of Water Rats', whose main aim was to help other 'pros' in distress as quickly and discreetly as possible, but whose particular pleasure was to indulge themselves on Sunday evenings in a room above the White Horse pub in Brixton. Dan, who was King Rat in 1891, 1892 and 1897, was very proud of his association with the Order and sang the anthem with pride as well as gusto:

This is the emblem of our Society
Each member acts with the greatest propriety,
Jolly old sports, to us they raise their hats,
A jolly lot of fellows are the Water Rats.
Rats! Rats! Rats.

Dan lost a lot of his money by going into management. He, Herbert Campbell, Harry Randall (who eventually succeeded Dan as the Lane's resident pantomime Dame), and another London comic, Fred Williams, decided that it might be profitable and interesting to open a music hall of their own. They took over a small seven-hundred seater called the Muntz Hall, just by Clapham Junction, refurbished it, renamed it the Grand Hall, Clapham, and gave it a rousing send-off by appearing there on the same bill in the first week. The hall was a success and prospered. Then they got more ambitious. They leased a hall in Croydon and called it the Empire. It did rather well too, so they bought a site at Walham Green and invited Frank Matcham, the celebrated theatre architect who was responsible for both the London Coliseum and the Hippodrome, to design it. They called it the Granville and it was a little gem: Dan was particularly proud of the interior decoration which featured faience work carried out by the Doultons! Next they built the Palace at Camberwell and a larger hall near their original hall in Clapham which they closed.

Then the trouble began. The proprietors and managers of all the big halls began to look askance at the suburban successes of this quartet of comedians, who were all very talented performers, but none of whom were experienced capitalists. The owners of the big halls eventually decided that the time had come to crush the new boys. They did so without difficulty. Every contract they made with an artiste had a barring clause in it which prevented them from appearing at any one of the quartet's four halls. According to Harry Randall,

> the tactics of these managers became very questionable. Artists would religiously turn up for their engagements, only to be promptly injuncted. Not only did they act thus, they so timed their injunction that it was not served till late on the Monday afternoon when all the bills were out and we were debarred from getting decent substitutes. We fought against it for a long time, but the attacking force was too powerful for us, and we slowly decayed.

Right could not fight might and the venture failed. It cost all four of them thousands of pounds and many of their friends, who had invested in the enterprise, lost considerable sums as well.

Even so, even after he had given away thousands and lost thousands, Dan still had a great deal of money to spend on himself. 'It may seem easy now, but I've had to dig for everything I've got.' And having dug and unearthed the pot of gold, he enjoyed spending it. While other artistes travelled from hall to hall in a hired hansom, Dan was able to move about London in style, travelling in his own brougham with his own coachman. When they first came to London, he and Lydia had shared a small room in Kennington. Even when they made their fortune, they still stayed south of the river, but they moved into rather more spacious and gracious surroundings. In 1898 they bought a substantial house called The Lodge at 56 Akerman Road in Brixton—the house still stands and is adorned by a London County Council plaque commemorating Dan: when it was unveiled on 12 April 1962 it was the first of the council's plaques to record the association of a house with a music hall star—and in 1901 moved into the splendour of Springfield House in Atkins Road in Balham, which is now a Convent called La Retraite.

Springfield was a large, detached house, with three acres of grounds, including paddocks and stabling for the three horses.

The coachman and his family lived over the stables in a flat and living in the house with the Leno family were the cook and two maids. Some found the décor of the interior of the house opulent, others thought it a trifle vulgar. No one failed to be impressed.

In *Fifty Years of a Londoner's Life* H. G. Hibbert recorded the first time he met Dan at Springfield: 'I was ushered into a wonderful drawing room, all yellow and green plush, and bronze figures, and marble vases, and flower-pots on bamboo tripods; so dimly lighted that I fell headlong across the skull of a tiger still attached to the skin forming the hearthrug. Dan came from his hiding place behind a screen, wreathed in smiles. "They mostly does that," he said.'

If Dan liked the opulence, Mrs. Leno adored it. Her upbringing had been hardly any more prosperous than Dan's and wealth pleased her without apparently spoiling her. At Springfield she was never happier than when supervising her two maids as they gave the precious Dresden china she loved to collect its dainty daily wash. She had given up her career at the beginning of 1888 and retired into a life of domesticity which she found thoroughly satisfying. She scorned the idea of having a nanny or governess to help her bring up their six children,* because she enjoyed her role as a mother. She enjoyed being 'Mrs. Dan Leno' too. She welcomed the attentions paid to her husband by the press and the public and when she went with the children to Drury Lane and sat in the Royal Box, with Jimmy Glover waiting in the orchestra pit with baton raised until she and her party were settled, she said she 'felt like royalty' and admitted finding the sensation a pleasant one. Dan was not a philanderer and, though he worked unceasingly and was often away from home, the marriage was regarded by them both as a success.

* There were six little Lenos: Georgina Louisa, born on 2 October 1884; John William, born on 16 April 1888; Ernest George, born on 26 May 1889; Sidney Paul, born on 31 July 1891; Herbert Dan, born on 3 May 1893; and May Lillian, born on 10 October 1895. Of the six, three—Ernest, Sidney and May—followed in their parents' footsteps. Of the three the best known was Sidney who borrowed his younger brother Herbert's second name (with permission) and called himself Dan Leno Junior.

The children did not see a great deal of their father. He rarely got home before two in the morning and never came down to have breakfast with them. The oldest was just twenty when he died, the youngest only nine, and though none of them got to know him well, they all remained absolutely loyal to his memory. When the children did see him, it was usually in the 'playroom', where he pursued the 'magnum opus of his hours of recreation', his 'panorama'. This was a vast canvas that could be rolled round mechanically and acted as a moving backcloth. When Dan, aided only by his children and Johnny Danvers, had completed it, the panorama took you round the world: from Liverpool Street Station to Mount Vesuvius, via darkest Africa, Prince's Street in Edinburgh and sundry other inconsequential ports of call.

Dan's idea when he launched himself on this enterprise was to provide some occupation for his elderly stepfather, thinking the old boy might be able to use it for a lecturing tour. However, Mr. Leno Senior's death having preceded the completion of the masterwork, Dan carried on for the sake of carrying on. From start to finish it took him twelve whole years to complete and when the job was done he rashly sold it to a ventriloquist known as Lieutenant Cole, but quickly bought it back again and kept it in full working order and mint condition until the end of his days.

Apart from painting—he sketched and water-coloured more than competently—Dan had few hobbies. He did a bit of carpentry and model-making. He was an accomplished exponent of the toy theatre. He dabbled in photography. He loved animals and kept rabbits and hens and ducks at Springfield, regarding them as his own very personal pets. He only played cricket and soccer for fun and for charity. Golf he avoided, but billiards he sometimes indulged in. He was an enthusiastic cyclist, he enjoyed walking and, now and again, he did a spot of gardening. But in his life there was little time for leisure: he devoted almost every waking hour to work.

CHAPTER SIX

The King's Jester

On Tuesday 26 November 1901, the impeccable Seymour Hicks, actor-manager and dramatist, later to be nicknamed the 'Admirable Crichton of the British stage' and knighted for his services to the theatre, his beautiful and, some said, even-more-talented wife, Ellaline Terriss, and the diminutive Dan Leno, travelled to Sandringham House in Norfolk to entertain the King. The occasion was the birthday of Her Royal Highness Princess Charles of Denmark and it was the first Command Performance of Edward VII's reign.

Mr. and Mrs. Hicks entertained the royal party with *Scrooge*, a one-act version of *A Christmas Carol*, and a musical duologue called *Papa's Wife*. Dan Leno held the floor for thirty-five minutes with two of his best-known songs, 'How to Buy a House' and 'The Huntsman', and a great deal of patter. The performance was, predictably, a splendid success. After it was over, Dan reported, 'The King, the Queen and the Prince of Wales all very kindly shook hands with me and told me how much they had enjoyed it. The Princess of Wales was just going to shake hands with me, when she looked at my face, and couldn't do it for some time, because she laughed so much. I wasn't intending to look funny—I was really trying to look dignified and courtly; but I suppose I couldn't help myself.'

To those who remember Queen Mary in later years, the picture of her getting the giggles is a shade improbable, but then there was something a little less than credible about several of the stories the indiscreet Dan gave to the press concerning his adventures at Sandringham. If Dan's version of the evening's events is to be believed in its entirety, it would appear that the little man had forgotten to bring the trousers that went with his dress suit and was obliged to borrow his dresser's blue serge trousers, which happened to be twice the size of his own and had to be kept in place with safety pins. Furthermore, he had no white tie and the one he borrowed was so long he had to tie it twice around his neck in an absurdly massive bow. Thus, having met the King and his family dressed, as he put it, like 'the corner-man of a nigger minstrel troupe', Dan decided to cool off in the royal gardens where he was promptly arrested in the shrubbery by a royal detective!

Whether the evening passed quite as fantastically as Dan would have had the world believe is uncertain, but what cannot be disputed is that the King presented Dan with a handsome jewelled tie-pin as a momento of the occasion. It was a singular tribute from a King to a mere comic from the halls and Dan was very conscious of the great honour done to him. So was his public. When he next appeared at the London Pavilion the audience stood and cheered. 'His Majesty has presented me with this very handsome diamond pin,' he told them, fumbling in his pockets to find it. He searched and searched and searched but, no, it had gone. He looked over the footlights bleakly, then, with a care-worn shrug of the shoulders, said, 'Well, you know how things are these days,' and held out his empty hands in an attempt to elicit their sympathy for his having had to pawn his royal bounty so quickly. Once the gag got a big laugh, he produced the pin. He held it up high as his adoring audience roared and roared.

From that moment on, unquestionably the king of jesters, Dan was known universally as 'the King's jester'. But, according to several of his friends, it was the moment too that marked the beginning of the end for Dan. 'It seems an extraordinary thing to say,' said Arthur Roberts, a good friend of his who was a big star on the halls and in the Lane pantomimes before Dan and whose career continued successfully right up to the 1920s, 'but I really believe that King Edward's kindness was the unconscious means of hastening Dan Leno's mind over the borderland of sanity. . . . Poor Dan had been fluttering outside the cage of the madhouse for some years, and the great honour and dignity which he received at the hands of the King just tilted the scales of divine injustice. He went inside.'

When Dan performed for the King at Sandringham he was a month away from his forty-first birthday. He died from a tumour of the brain less than three years later. There were distressing rumours at the time about the origin of the tumour, but the precise cause was not established and never will be: none of the medical papers relating to his illness has survived. Dan himself used to attribute his 'brain trouble' to 'a fall off a bicycle'. Whatever the cause, the effect was dramatic: from Christmas 1901 he became increasingly unstable, he was advised to take plenty of 'rest' and went to various seaside resorts and private nursing homes to do so. His condition continued to deteriorate and eventually his wife had no alternative but to agree to his being taken away for treatment. At the turn of the century there was little understanding of the nature of mental illnesses ('brain fag' was the corporate term used in polite circles), still less of the complex symptoms of a brain tumour. There was no known cure and, though palliatives were available for the relief of pain and as much rest as possible was prescribed, there was no real treatment.

Dan's past way of life had not been conducive to good health, mental or physical. From the age of four he had been an itinerant performer, always on the move, without a proper home, usually living in conditions of dire and sometimes of abject poverty. From the age of twenty-four as one of his friends put it, 'he worked himself steadily into the grave'. Many music hall artistes gave their all to their work and not a few, like Dan, ended by sacrificing their lives to it. He was an obsessive worker and, as the years went by and his fame and wealth increased, the obsession seemed to grow: ironically, the greater his security the more insecure he felt, the louder his audiences cheered the more convinced he became that 'nobody cares for me—nobody!', the less he needed to work the more he felt compelled to.

Any kind of stage performance is physically exhausting (and the exhaustion is quite disproportionate to the actual amount of time spent on stage) and to his own act, which was extraordinarily

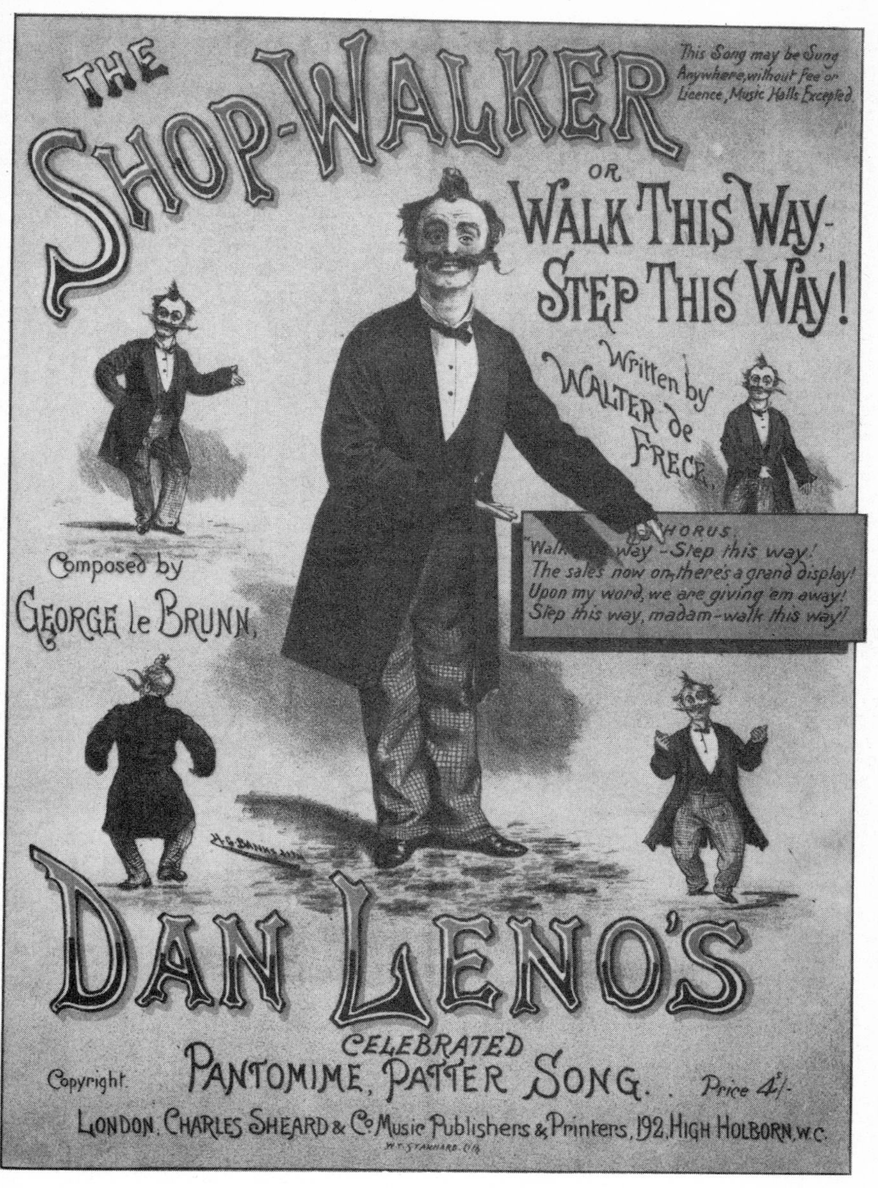

9 Dan's 'Songs': The Shopwalker

10a The Railway Guard

10b Nevermore

11a The Bandit

11b The Beefeater

12 Going Out of Town – simply signed 'Leno', the grandiose autograph he affected towards the end of his life

HELLO! I'VE BEEN WAITING FOR YOU. PAY YOUR HALFPENNY AND LET'S BE OFF.

DAN LENO'S COMIC JOURNAL

½

No. 1. Vol. 1
WEEK ENDING
February 26, 1898.

"ONE TOUCH OF LENO MAKES THE WHOLE WORLD GRIN."

EVERY TUESDAY.

A PEEP AT THE EDITORIAL DEN.

My dear friends,—Greeting. I am informed by everyone I know that the funniest thing I have ever done is to become editor of a funny paper. Well, that's just how it ought to be; otherwise the pains I have taken in getting out my first number would have been used to better advantage for glazing purposes. You can read all about my staff—whose portraits appear above—inside. The telegrams of congratulation from the Emperor of Germany and other crowned heads of Europe on the appearance of my Comic Journal have been crowded out to make room for the Police News. They will be published next week; so till next Tuesday, ta, ta, and be good.

Herewith my hand and quill, Yours ever, Dan Leno

13 Issue Number One of *Dan Leno's Comic Journal*, 26 February 1898

14a Dan and Herbert Campbell edit *The Sun* for 1 April 1902

14b The King's Jester wearing the King's pin

15a The drawing room at Springfield House in Balham

15b Dan Leno at home

15c Mrs Leno at home

DAILY MIRROR, Tuesday, November 1, 1904.

Buy a Copy of "The World and His Wife" To-day.

½d.

Daily Mirror

A BEAUTIFUL KEEPSAKE. (See page 6.)

No. 311. | Registered at the G.P.O. as a Newspaper. | TUESDAY, NOVEMBER 1, 1904. | One Halfpenny.

DEATH OF MR. DAN LENO, THE FAMOUS COMEDIAN.

Mr. Leno as a widow in a pantomime.

One of his most characteristic poses.—(Denton and Co.)

Mr. Leno as a shop-walker—(Photo. Co.)

The last photograph of the famous comedian, taken a few days ago.—(Denton and Co.)

Mr. Leno as an editor.—(Haines.)

Gardening, his favourite pastime. — (Foulsham and Banfield.)

At home with two of his pets. — (Foulsham and Banfield.)

16 The front page of the *Daily Mirror* on Tuesday 1 November 1904

physical anyway, Dan brought a manic energy of his own. What made matters worse, of course, was that he did not expend his energy exclusively on the stage: he was always on the go. When he was not required during the pantomime rehearsals, he did not rest in his dressing-room: he entertained the rest of the cast. When he toured in *Orlando Dando* for Milton Bode a special saloon car was provided on the train for his private use: he was rarely in it. He preferred to be in an ordinary carriage entertaining the 'boys'. In London he would appear at three and sometimes four music halls in an evening and provide encores whenever they were asked for—and they were asked for every time. When he appeared in provincial music halls the audiences rarely let him leave the stage until he had done ten of his songs, complete with patter.

J. Hickory Wood in his biography of Dan gave a sample day in the life of Leno 'as a fairly typical example of what he was able to endure'. In the morning he travelled to Dudley in Staffordshire to ceremonially open a new music hall. Having made his speech and done his turn, he returned to London where he performed at a charity matinée 'where a delighted audience declined to part with him until he had sung six songs'. Next he attended a charity dinner, half-way through which he had to absent himself and make his way to the Pavilion Music Hall to undertake his first professional engagement of the day. Having done his turn at the Pavilion he went back to the charity dinner to make his speech there. 'After this, he was free to go home, and for all anybody knew, to rest. But he had not yet had any time to look at his correspondence, and as every day brought with it a pile of letters that he invariably looked through and answered personally, the birds in his garden were up and singing long before Dan went to bed and dreamt of a lot of things he had to do when he woke.'

What Hickory Wood failed to mention, not surprisingly since he was writing only months after Dan's death, was that between finishing his official duties and making his way home, Dan would regularly repair to the Trocadero for a late supper and then go on to less salubrious hostelries for yet more liquid refreshment. Dan, the son of one heavy drinker and the stepson of another, developed a drink problem that eventually became chronic. Drink has long been accepted as one of the occupational hazards of the entertainment business and, at first, friends took lightly the fact that he could so easily be tempted to have a drink 'on small provocation with comparative strangers' in Johnny Danvers's phrase. Eventually they began to realise the gravity of the situation and did what they could to save him from himself. H. Chance Newton, a music hall performer turned theatrical journalist, was one of those who knew him well 'in the unhappy time when, thanks to well-meaning but foolish "treating" friends, he had become too fond of the often devastating "another with me" habit.' Newton did his best to curb his alcoholic excesses: 'Many a time was I able—when other equally loyal friends had failed—to get Dan away from his "bar" companions both of the well-meaning kind and of the ear-biting and slavering sort. Many a night, for months together, did I "capture" Dan when he had finished his night's work, and carry him off straight away to his home.'

Inevitably his drinking began to affect his performance. So, too, in a different but no less insidious way, did his increasing deafness. It had its amusing moments—at a rehearsal for *Bluebeard* in 1901 Dan was left stuck up a tower on the stage for twenty minutes because he had not heard the producer announce the break in rehearsals; at the end of the run of *Mother Goose* in 1903 he was presented with a beautiful service of silver plate by the management but not having heard a word of Arthur Collins's tribute to him when Collins unveiled the silver plate and the company applauded, Dan rose to his feet and said: 'Governor, it's a magnificent present! I congratulate you, and you deserve it!'—but on the whole it made life difficult both for him and those working with him. It was a special problem for Jimmy Glover and his orchestra at the Lane: Dan's voice had never been a big one, so while needing to keep the music sufficiently 'down' for him to be heard, they had to keep it sufficiently 'up' for him to hear the tune.

In 1901 and 1902, as his deafness, which was one of the symptoms of his general condition, got worse and his drinking increased, he became more temperamental than ever. He would throw terrible scenes and then be overcome with pitiful remorse and regret. Within the space of one hour and in the same company he could become totally hysterical then strangely subdued. His generosity, which had always been reckless, now became lunatic. He distributed coins, notes, pieces of jewellery even, not just to the beggars and street boys and frauds who hung around the stage doors waiting to catch him, but to complete strangers. And whereas he had always been an enthusiast for costume and make-up and enjoyed dressing up as some of the great figures of history to win first prize at a fancy dress ball, he now yearned to portray those great figures on the stage—and was convinced he could do it.

Eventually, early in 1903, shortly after the end of the run of *Mother Goose*, the delusions of grandeur overwhelmed him. One evening, at about 10.30, he made his way to the home of Constance Collier who was then at the height of her fame as Sir Herbert Beerbohm Tree's leading lady at His Majesty's. Neither Miss Collier, who was only twenty-five at the time, nor her mother were in, but the maid showed Dan into the sitting room where he sat and waited for the ladies to return. 'It must have been about one o'clock when we put the key in the latch. We usually went straight to our bedrooms, but something told me to open the sitting-room door. There was no light in the room, except from the window, which let in a little bit of moon. To our utter amazement, Dan Leno was sitting on the sofa! I had never met Dan Leno, but I had adored him from afar since I was a little girl. My mother had taken me to see him in every successive pantomime in the following years. He was the greatest star in London at that time, certainly the most brilliant comedian I have ever seen, and he had an amazing quality of pathos. His eyes were beautiful, like the eyes of a wounded animal or a great tragedian. They were deep-sunken and looked as if they would fill with tears at any moment. They were like Mrs. Patrick Campbell's eyes. His voice was low and husky and he was small and delicate looking, with a very slender and fragile body. . . .

'When I came towards him, he took my hand eagerly. He was trembling with excitement. My mother was standing behind him, laughing from sheer pleasure at seeing him, and I was smiling too.

We were utterly amazed! As he began to speak something in his face arrested me, and I frowned at my mother. Then began the most pathetic half-hour, almost, I can remember. . . .

'He said he was the son of a Scottish marquis, and that his mother had been a housemaid in his father's great mansion somewhere in the north. He was nine years old when he tramped up to London with her, and they walked all those miles in the bitter winter. He sang outside village public-houses for a few coppers to get their food, and they ate snow to quench their thirst as they tramped along the frozen roads! It took them nearly a month to get down from Scotland, walking all the way.

'He told he of his life of direst poverty in London, of his struggles until he began to be known and fame came to him at last. All the time he was holding my hand in the most painful grip. My arm was nearly paralysed. And then he told me the ambition of his life was to play Shakespeare, and that he had the most profound admiration and friendship for Sir Henry Irving. He had seen everything he had done for many years, and for the past six months he had watched me in *Ben Hur* and *Ulysses* and *The Eternal City*, time after time, sitting in the gallery or at the back of the pit with his collar turned up so that few would recognise him. How excited they would have been had they known they were sitting next to their idol! He said he had saved up enough money to fulfil the ambition of his life—he wanted me to make a contract to play in Shakespeare with him for five years. . . .

'Some time before he had played a scene from *Richard III* at a matinée. I wasn't present, but many people told me that he had started seriously, but when people began to laugh he had turned it into a joke. Now, looking at him, I knew his ambition to be a true one. Some strange barrier had been let down in his brain and he was speaking out—at last. . . .

'I didn't know what to do. There was no telephone in my flat; I couldn't get help from anybody, and I knew he was very ill. I took him down the stairs and told him to see Herbert Tree in the morning at the theatre. I thought if I put him off in this way I should be able to explain to Sir Herbert and get him to help me.

'When we got downstairs there was an old coachman, sitting

on the box of a one-horse brougham, smoking a pipe, waiting for him. He drove off quite happily, relying on my promise. I felt a traitor as I stood there watching the carriage drive away. I shall never forget his little, eager face as he looked out of the window at me. He was so content, so radiantly happy that he was to play the great roles—Richard III and Hamlet! I felt somehow I was betraying him. I think I was the first person to whom he ever really told that secret ambition—the innermost hope of his heart.

'I got to rehearsal early next morning, but Dan Leno was before me. He had been there for about two hours. Lots of people were standing about the stage door, members of the company, stage hands, etc., all with grinning faces. Everybody loved Dan Leno. The door-keeper had an odd look on his face—a cross between puzzlement and delight. He instinctively felt the strangeness in Dan Leno's manner, although he was making everybody scream with laughter. He had insisted on giving the old man money to buy himself a silk top hat to wait on Sir Herbert and me. The others were very amused, but the door-keeper was a wise old man!

'Dan Leno had been busy making several imaginary contracts with the smaller members of the company, writing them out carefully on bits of paper and signing them! He had given handfuls of money to the paperboys in the Haymarket, who were delightedly crowding round the stage door, watching his every antic, thinking he was doing it all for fun.

'We were rehearsing a serious one-act play at the time, *The Man Who Was*, and I was the heroine. Sir Herbert was not at rehearsal, and I had been unable to communicate with him or tell him of my fears, but I managed to get hold of the call-boy and asked him to warn Sir Herbert, as he came in, that I thought Mr. Leno was very ill. He seemed so well in health and was so amusing that the call-boy asked me to repeat my message.

'Then followed an agonising half-hour. While I was rehearsing, wherever I went Dan Leno accompanied me. If I sat down, he sat too; if I stood, he stood beside me; if I walked, he was at my side. The company giggled wildly, thinking it a huge joke.

'Presently Sir Herbert appeared with his manager. The call-boy had given him my message. He made a sign to me and took Dan Leno into the stalls to talk matters over, and we continued to rehearse.

'Then a strange time followed. I could see Dan Leno and Sir Herbert in the empty stalls, talking and talking—staring into each other's eyes. Our theatre manager was with them, but Tree sent him away on some errand or other. (I afterwards found he had sent for Mr. Leno's manager to come and take care of him). . . . Presently the manager appeared with two men, and Dan Leno shook hands and went away quite happily.

'When Sir Herbert came on the stage he beckoned me towards him and said he feared something was seriously wrong—we hardly dared speak that dreadful word between us. He was very pale and his eyes were sunken—the fading light of inspiration was on his face, as if he had seen a vision that was past. He was silent for a moment, staring into space. Then he said: "If this is madness, what is the use of being sane? If ever he plays Richard III—it will be the greatest performance of the part we have seen." Then he pulled himself together and looked at the people on the stage. "Let's go back to work. How dull normal people are!"

'We had a late rehearsal that afternoon and other things crowded my mind, but when I got home about five o'clock what was my amazement to find Dan Leno awaiting me. He had eluded his manager with that strange cunning of a twisted mind. He had a jewel-case in his hand with a diamond plaque. The stones were wonderful—it was a very valuable piece. He loved jewels, I believe, and always bought them. I was foolish enough to refuse the plaque.

'He told me that Tree had agreed to all the terms, and there was nothing left but to sign the contract, and he would send the information to the papers.

'I didn't know what to do—I didn't realise that Sir Herbert had warned the papers not to publish any statement that might be sent in regarding my future appearances; I didn't want the story to get out! I fenced with Mr. Leno for a little while, and then refused the offer. I have never seen such crushing disappointment on anybody's face as he said: "You don't believe that I can play Shakespeare, then?"

'I tried to explain that there were other reasons, but it was no good, and he left me with the tears pouring down his face.

'He gave the diamonds to a barmaid on his way home. . . . Two days afterwards he was taken to a nursing-home.'

He spent several months in Camberwell House in Camberwell, under the care of a Dr. Savage who prescribed 'peace and quiet' and a little water-colouring. Arthur Roberts saw some of the pictures Dan painted in the home 'in a collection of works of art produced by fellow lunatics. It was a very terrible exhibition. There were hints and glimpses everywhere of misguided genius and there was evidence on all hands that worked at the dictation of abnormal and tortured minds.' Dan, deluded as he was, knew what was happening to him—on his second day at the home he pointed out that the hall clock must be wrong and on being told it was quite right, remarked, 'If it's quite right, what's it doing here?'—and didn't like it. He made several attempts to get home and once or twice succeeded. He was taken back each time.

Towards the end of August, Dr. Savage concluded that the patient was well enough to be allowed home. The press, which had been full of rumours as to the nature of his illness, gave considerable coverage to 'Dan Leno's recovery' and welcoming verses like this one appeared in several papers:

Dan Leno is better,—Thank God is the cry,—
Without him, we know, much stage humour would die.
He has been very ill and a sad time has led,
And once, it was rumoured, Dan Leno was dead.

Such is not the case I am much pleased to say,
For our artiste still lives and improves day by day,
And soon we may see him, and hear him again,
At the Oxford, Tivoli and at old Drury Lane.

That Dan would be well enough to appear in the pantomime at the Lane was still in doubt and Arthur Collins, who had been warned by Dr. Savage that Dan might be well enough but might equally well suffer a relapse between September and December, took the precaution of engaging Harry Randall to appear in Dan's place, playing Mary the Cook, with Herbert Campbell, continuing as usual as the other principal comedian, playing Queen Spritely. In the event, when the time came for the start of rehearsals, Dan was deemed fit enough to appear. The parts were reshuffled so that Herbert Campbell became a new character called King Sollum and Dan, who was given much less to do in the show, became Queen Spritely.

Under the circumstances, the rehearsals went well. Dan worked quietly and conscientiously, trying to regain his old form and doing his best to keep off the drink. He did lapse once or twice and disappeared to a bar—as often as not the canteen under the London Hippodrome—with a couple of old cronies, but on the whole, by dint of self-discipline and careful management by Arthur Collins, he stayed the course.

The first night came and Dan went on. The moment the audience heard his introductory music they began to cheer. The moment he appeared at the gates, sumptuously attired as Queen Spritely, they got to their feet and roared. The standing ovation lasted a full five minutes. Dan Leno was back and all was right with the world! 'Not only did Mr. Leno take part in an entertainment which legions of playgoers would have great difficulty in recognising as an entertainment without him', wrote one critic the following day, echoing the sentiments of all, 'but it was evident continuously, at any rate at every critical juncture, that he was his old and best self.'

The truth of the matter was rather different. Dan, never at his easiest on first nights, had certainly survived the ordeal, but only just. Repeatedly he fluffed his lines and in both his 'big' scenes the other artistes had to rescue him by feeding him his cues. Nonetheless the public was delighted to see their old idol back on stage again and the pantomime was a great success: it ran for over twelve weeks and for the first six weeks there was a matinée every day. Each performance lasted four hours and as the weeks went by the strain began to tell on Dan. Off-stage he started throwing scenes and locking himself in his dressing-room. On stage he became even less sure of himself: fumbling for his lines, missing his cues, speaking inaudibly.

On the last night of *Humpty Dumpty*, at the end of the show Dan and Herbert Campbell stepped forward and, hands clasped, sang this duet:

> In the panto of old Drury Lane
> We have both come together again,
>   And we hope to appear
>   For many a year
> In the panto of old Drury Lane.

It was a wish neither of them lived to fulfil. Herbert Campbell, who, apart from Johnny Danvers, was Dan's closest friend, died after an accident on 19 July 1904 at the age of fifty-seven. And Dan, after making a few last pathetic appearances at seaside resorts—he thought the air would do him good—and at the London Pavilion, where he had once been so brilliant and now could not even recall the words of his own songs, soon followed his old friend to the grave. During the summer his condition had got dramatically worse. His decline was accelerated by the news of Campbell's death. He died in Lydia's arms on 31 October 1904.

Dan's death came as a shock, but not as a surprise. 'So little and frail a lantern could not long harbour so big a flame', wrote Max Beerbohm in the *Saturday Review*. The news was national news. The *Daily Mirror* devoted its entire front page to the story. The *Daily Telegraph* wrote, 'There was only one "Dan". His methods were inimitable; his face was indeed his fortune . . . Who has seen him in any of his disguises and has failed to laugh?' All the obituaries echoed the same sentiments.

The morning of the funeral, 8 November, was sunny but bitterly cold. Large crowds gathered silently outside Dan's house and lined the three miles of the funeral route. The traffic was halted. The shops were closed. Many eyes were filled with tears as the sad procession made its way towards Lambeth Cemetery in Tooting. The hearse bearing the tiny coffin was escorted by eight 'King Rats' and followed by a hundred carriages and cabs filled with relatives and friends and admirers. The Reverend Canon Curtis, vicar of the Church of the Ascension, Balham Hill, conducted the service. 'What is the meaning of this vast congregation and of the gathering of the thousands outside?' he asked in his address. 'I hope, I believe, that it is not mere curiosity that has brought the people together, but the desire to pay respect to the mortal remains of a great genius.'

The plate on the coffin bore the inscription:

GEORGE GALVIN
('Dan Leno')
Who Entered into Rest, 31st Oct., 1904
Aged 43 Years

The ceremony at the graveside and the actual burial were intended to be private, but the pressure from the hushed throng of people massed outside the graveyard was so great that the lock on the gates to the cemetery broke and Dan's public surged slowly in and surrounded the grave. Their idol was dead and the world was a sadder place.

And now, almost three-quarters of a century after his death, what is left of the legendary Leno? Little more than the legend really: a few scratchy records, a plaque on his house in Brixton, a small self-portrait in the National Portrait Gallery, a bust at Drury Lane, the Champion Clog Dancer of the World's belt at his son's house in Surrey but not the King's tie-pin—that either disappeared when Springfield was auctioned or he gave it away during his last illness. They say his ghost still haunts the Lane—Stanley Lupino once saw it—but very few of the people who fill the theatre today, and whose grandparents and great-grandparents adored and admired him above all other entertainers, have even heard of the name Dan Leno. His star shone brighter than Marie Lloyd's, though far more people still know her name. And yet, and yet, to those who saw him, he was—yes, he really, truly *was*—'the funniest man on earth'. 'I think I see some of my readers', wrote Max Beerbohm,'—such of them as never saw Dan Leno—raising their eyebrows. Nor do I blame them. Nor do I blame myself for failing to recreate that which no howsoever ingenious literary artist could recreate for you. I can only echo the old heart-cry "Si ipsum audissetis!" Some day, no doubt, the phonograph and the bioscope will have been so adjusted to each other that we shall see and hear past actors and singers as well as though they were alive before us. I wish Dan Leno could have been thus immortalised. No actor of our time deserved immortality so well as he.'

Dan Leno on Stage

As well as making thousands of appearances in music hall, between 1886 and his death in 1904 Dan Leno appeared in eighteen pantomimes and four musical comedies.

Boxing Day 1886, The Royal Surrey Theatre, Blackfriars Road: *Jack and the Beanstalk* by George Conquest and Henry Spry, with Dan Leno as Dame Durden.

Boxing Day 1887, The Royal Surrey Theatre, Blackfriars Road: *Sindbad and the Little Old Man of the Sea* by George Conquest and Henry Spry, with Dan Leno as Tinpanz.

November 1888, The Royal Strand Theatre: *Atalanta* by George P. Hawtrey, with Dan Leno as Leontes. (The burlesque opened on 17 November, but Dan did not join the cast until the end of the month.)

Boxing Day 1888, Theatre Royal, Drury Lane: *Babes in the Wood* by Augustus Harris, E. L. Blanchard and Harry Nicholls, with Dan Leno as the Baroness.

Boxing Day 1889, Theatre Royal, Drury Lane: *Jack and the Beanstalk* by Harry Nicholls and Augustus Harris, with Dan Leno as Mrs. Simpson.

Boxing Day 1890, Theatre Royal, Drury Lane: *Beauty and the Beast* by W. Yardley and Augustus Harris, with Dan Leno as Mr. Lombarde Streete.

Boxing Day 1891, Theatre Royal, Drury Lane: *Humpty Dumpty* by Harry Nicholls and Augustus Harris, with Dan Leno as the Queen of Hearts.

Boxing Day 1892, Theatre Royal, Drury Lane: *Little Bo-Peep, Little Red Riding-Hood and Hop o' My Thumb* by Augustus Harris and Wilton Jones, with Dan Leno as Daddy Thumb.

Boxing Day 1893, Theatre Royal, Drury Lane: *Robinson Crusoe* by Harry Nicholls and Augustus Harris, with Dan Leno as Mrs. Crusoe.

Boxing Day 1894, Theatre Royal, Drury Lane: *Dick Whittington* by Augustus Harris, Cecil Raleigh and Henry Hamilton, with Dan Leno as Idle Jack.

Boxing Day 1895, Theatre Royal, Drury Lane: *Cinderella* by Augustus Harris, Cecil Raleigh and Arthur Sturgess, with Dan Leno as the Baroness.

Boxing Day 1896, Theatre Royal, Drury Lane: *Aladdin* by Arthur Sturgess and H. Leonard, with Dan Leno as Mrs. Twankey.

Boxing Day 1897, Theatre Royal, Drury Lane: *The Babes in the Wood* by Arthur Sturgess and Arthur Collins, with Dan Leno as Reggie.

1 August 1898, The Grand Theatre, Fulham, followed by a tour: *Orlando Dando*

by Basil Hood and Walter Slaughter, with Dan Leno as Orlando Dando.
Boxing Day 1898, Theatre Royal, Drury Lane: *The Forty Thieves* by Arthur Sturgess and Arthur Collins, with Dan Leno as Abdallah.
9 October 1899, Theatre Royal, Glasgow, followed by a tour: *In Gay Piccadilly!* by George R. Sims and Clarence Corri, with Dan Leno as Aubrey Honeybun.
Boxing Day 1899, Theatre Royal, Drury Lane: *Jack and the Beanstalk* by Arthur Sturgess and Arthur Collins, with Dan Leno as Dame Trot.
Boxing Day 1900, Theatre Royal, Drury Lane: *The Sleeping Beauty and the Beast* by J. Hickory Wood and Arthur Collins, with Dan Leno as Queen Ravia.
Boxing Day 1901, Theatre Royal, Drury Lane: *Bluebeard* by J. Hickory Wood and Arthur Collins, with Dan Leno as Sister Anne.
21 July 1902, Stratford Borough Theatre, followed by a tour: *Mr. Wix of Wickham* by Herbert Darnley, with Dan Leno as Mr. Wix.
Boxing Day 1902, Theatre Royal, Drury Lane: *Mother Goose* by J. Hickory Wood and Arthur Collins with Dan Leno as Mother Goose.
Boxing Day 1903, Theatre Royal, Drury Lane: *Humpty Dumpty* by J. Hickory Wood and Arthur Collins, with Dan Leno as Queen Spritely.

Dan Leno on Record

Dan Leno made twenty-nine records for the Gramophone and Typewriter Company just after the turn of the century. Brian Rust has been able to identify and date the recordings and I am most grateful to him for kindly allowing me to publish the results of his research. In the list that follows the numbers in the first column are the recording numbers and the numbers in the last column are the issue numbers.

Recorded at four sessions during November 1901

1066	*Who Does the House Belong To?*	GC-2-2518
1067	*The Mocking Bird*	GC-1204
1082	*The Tower Of London*	GC-2435
1084	*The May Day Fireman*	GC-2436
1091	*Where Are You Going To, My Pretty Maid?*	GC-1207
1092	*My Wife's Relations*	GC-1205
1093	*The Huntsman*	GC-2-2515
1094	*The Grass Widower*	GC-2-2516
1095	*Clever Mr. Green*	GC-2-2517
1096	*McGlockell's Men*	GC-1206
1127	*Poppies*	GC-2-2530
1128	*Mrs. Kelly*	GC-2-2531
1129	*The Tower of London* (re-make)	GC-2435
1130	Unknown title	Unissued

Recorded on 6 March 1903

3222/3-R	*The Hard-Boiled Egg*	GC-2-2807
3224/5	*Going to the Races*	GC-2-2808

Recorded on 16 April 1903

3478/9	*The Shopwalker*	GC-2-2830
3480/1	*The Muffin Man*	GC-2-2831
3462/3	*Spiritualism*	GC-1243
3484/5	*Wait Till I'm His Father*	GC-2-2832

Recorded on 17 April 1903

3487/8	*The Fortune Teller*	GC-2-2854
3489/90	*The Diamond Ring*	GC-2-2833
3491/2	*The Swimming Master*	GC-2-2855
3484/5	*The Lecturer*	Unissued
3496/7	*Dan Leno's Clog Dance*	Unissued

All twenty-five of the recordings listed above were made as ten-inch records. At the beginning of 1903, Dan also made four twelve-inch records, most probably at the recording session on 6 March:

43-R	*I Am Waiting For Him Tonight*	02006
46-R	*The Robin*	01000
47-R	*Going To The Races*	02001
50-R	*The Huntsman*	02005

Acknowledgements

Of the trio of people who have been of most help to me in the preparation of this book, only one is still alive—but he is very much alive. Herbert Leno, at eighty-four, is Dan Leno's sole surviving son, and my debt to him is enormous. Not only have he and his charming daughter, Audrey Leno, been most helpful and hospitable: they have also given me complete access to the family's papers, press cuttings and photographs. They wish to make it clear that they do not associate themselves with the last Chapter of the book, the responsibility for which is mine alone.

J. Hickory Wood and Gerald Forsyth are the other two to whom I am most indebted. Hickory Wood, who died in 1913, was responsible for the 'book' of the last four of the Drury Lane pantomimes in which Dan Leno appeared and was the author of a delightful biography of Dan, which Methuen & Co. published in 1905. Since he was not only a friend of Dan's who worked closely with him during the last five years of his life, but also heard all the tales of Dan's youth from Johnny Danvers and Dan himself and recounted them much as he was told them, and since Dan's widow (who, incidentally, married 'Serini the Contortionist' a few years after Dan's death and became Mrs. Charles Best) always maintained that Hickory Wood's biography was a very reliable source, I have drawn heavily on it, most particularly in Chapters One and Two where I have reproduced several of Hickory Wood's stories of Dan's childhood adventures virtually verbatim.

Gerald Forsyth, who died much more recently, was a special kind of pantomime enthusiast who over the years built up a remarkable library of pantomime scripts. In 1973 I acquired his collection, which includes all the pantomimes in which Dan Leno appeared, and without which Chapter Four could not have been written.

Naturally, I have also drawn on all the books listed in the bibliography and I would like to thank the Bodley Head for their kind permission to reproduce the extract from Constance Collier's autobiography, *Harlequinade*, which appears in Chapter Six.

Finally, there are many organisations and individuals to whom I must extend my thanks for the time and willing co-operation they have generously given me, most especially the B.B.C. Sound Archives, Dudley Chapman, Daniel

Farson, Richard Findlater, Alan Gallop, Stephen Gleason, Richard Goolden, Gerard Heath, George Hoare, Roy Hudd, Philip Ingram, Derek Leask, Rowland Lindup, Constance Luttrell, Ray Mackender, Raymond Mander and Joe Mitchenson, David Mayer, Peter Moore, Max Tyler and George Nash, Tony Latham and Jennifer Aylmer of the Theatre Museum at the Victoria and Albert Museum. Obviously, the responsibility for any sins of omission or commission must be laid at my door, not theirs.

Bibliography

Max Beerbohm, *Around Theatres*, Rupert Hart-Davis, 1924.
Dion Clayton Calthrop, *Music Hall Nights*, John Lane the Bodley Head, 1925.
D. F. Cheshire, *Music Hall in Britain*, David and Charles, 1974.
Constance Collier, *Harlequinade*, John Lane the Bodley Head, 1929.
Peter Cotes, *George Robey*, Cassell, 1972.
M. Willson Disher, *Clowns and Pantomimes*, Constable, 1925.
M. Willson Disher, *Winkles and Champagne*, Batsford, 1938.
Brian Dobbs, *Drury Lane*, Cassell, 1972.
Daniel Farson, *Marie Lloyd and Music Hall*, Tom Staceau1972.
S. T. Felstead, *Stars Who Made the Halls*, T. Werner L rie, 1946.
John Fisher, *Funny Way to be a Hero*, Frederick Muller,1973.
Peter Gammond, *Your Own, Your Very Own*, Ian Allan, 1971.
H. G. Hibbert, *Fifty Years of a Londoner's Life*, Grant Richards, 1916.
Seymour Hicks, *Vintage Years*, Cassell, 1943.
Peter Honri, *Working the Halls*, Saxon House, 1973.
Diana Howard, *London Theatres and Music Halls 1850–1950*, Thə Library Association, 1970.
Naomi Jacob, *Our Marie*, Hutchinson, 1936.
George Le Roy, *Music Hall Stars of the Nineties*, British Technical and General Press, 1952.
Stanley Lupino, *From the Stocks to the Stars*, Hutchinson, 1934.
Colin MacInnes, *Sweet Saturday Night*, MacGibbon and Kee, 1967.
W. Macqueen-Pope, *The Melodies Linger On*, W. H. Allen, 1950.
W. Macqueen-Pope, *Pillars of Drury Lane*, Hutchinson, 1955.
Raymond Mander and Joe Mitchenson, *British Music Hall*, Studio Vista, 1965.
Raymond Mander and Joe Mitchenson, *Pantomime*, Peter Davies, 1973.
G. J. Mellor, *The Northern Music Hall*, Frank Graham, 1970.
W. H. Morton and H. Chance Newton, *Sixty Years' Stage Service*, Gale and Polden, 1905.
H. Chance Newton, *Idols of the 'Halls'*, Heath Cranton, 1928.
Harry Randall, *H.R. Old Time Comedian*, Sampson Lowe, 1931.
Ada Reeve, *Take it for a Fact*, Heinemann, 1954.
Arthur Roberts, *Fifty Years of Spoof*, John Lane the Bodley Head, 1927.

G. F. Scotson-Clark, with an introduction by George Gamble, *The 'Halls'*, T. Fisher Unwin, 1901.
Clement Scott, *The Drama of Yesterday and Today*, Macmillan, 1899.
Harold Scott, *The Early Doors*, Nicholson and Watson, 1946.
Ernest Short, *Fifty Years of Vaudeville*, Eyre and Spottiswoode, 1946.
Ernest Short, *Sixty Years of Theatre*, Eyre and Spottiswoode, 1951.
A. E. Wilson, *Pantomime Pageant*, Stanley Paul, 1946.
A. E. Wilson, *The Story of Pantomime*, Home and Van Thal, 1949.
A. E. Wilson, *Prime Minister of Mirth*, Odhams Press, 1956.
Georgie Wood, *I Had to be 'Wee'*, Hutchinson, 1948.
J. Hickory Wood, *Dan Leno*, Methuen, 1905.

Index